ENDORSEMENTS

Do you know the plan God has for your future? Are you aware that you are the developer of your future? In this book, *Shaping Your Future,* my good friend Barry Bennett identifies the clear Biblical principles that are involved with you learning to bring forth your future in the kingdom. This is a must read for all who desire to fulfill the will and plan of God for your life.

—Greg Mohr,
Executive Director of A.R.M.I.
(the Association of Related Ministries International)
and Post Education Development at Charis Bible College

To me, Barry Bennett is a powerhouse teacher and such an important figure in the body of Christ today! I am thrilled about this book and his expertise on faith, the power of our words, and reaching the future God has promised for us. Several years ago, I heard him preach a message on The Gospel of Clichés and was so impacted by it, that I had my entire staff listen to it! So many people fall in the trap of saying religious clichés and I love that Barry breaks these down and explains why many of them aren't scriptural and go against the faith needed to shape your future.

—Pastor Lawson Perdue,
Senior Pastor of Charis Christian Center, Colorado Springs, CO

SHAPING
YOUR
FUTURE

Harrison
House

Shippensburg, PA

Harrison House Books by Barry Bennett

He Healed Them All

Did God Do This To Me?

BARRY BENNETT

SHAPING
— *YOUR* —
FUTURE

Releasing Your
Destiny Through the
Power of the Seed

Published by Harrison House Publishers
Shippensburg, PA 17257

Cover design by Eileen Rockwell

ISBN 13 TP: 978-1-6803-1552-3

ISBN 13 eBook: 978-1-6803-1553-0

ISBN 13 HC: 978-1-6803-1555-4

ISBN 13 LP: 978-1-6803-1554-7

For Worldwide Distribution, Printed in the U.S.A.

2 3 4 5 6 7 8 / 25 24 23 22 21

CONTENTS

FOREWORD

BARRY Bennett is a living example of the seed of God's Word shaping your future. I've only known Barry and his wife Betty Kay for 14 years but I recognize the maturity in them that only God's Word can bring. When Barry first came to us at AWM and Charis Bible College, he humbly did whatever we asked him to do. He never told us that he had been through Bible College, a missionary in Chile, and directed a Spanish speaking Bible College. He never promoted himself.

He simply let the seed of God's Word grow and mature in him till everyone saw the fruit. We asked him to take a chapel service in Charis and it was amazing! The students gave him a standing ovation and requested more of the CD's of his teaching than anyone who had come through the college to that date. We gave him more opportunities and it wasn't long before he was a regular in the college and even rose to leadership.

When Barry ministers it is evident that he has a fresh word from the Lord that isn't just parroting someone else. He spends lots of time in God's Word. That's what this book is about. God's Word is like a seed that when planted, given the right conditions and time, just brings forth fruit effortlessly. God's Word is alive and if you will let it live in you, it will produce the supernatural fruit only God can give.

Although God's Word is a miraculous seed, it has to be mixed with faith for it to profit you (Hebrews 4:2) and faith is based on knowledge (2 Peter 1:3-4). Barry shares a lifetime of knowledge and experience with you in this book that will enable you to let faith rise in your heart and activate the miraculous power in the seed of God's Word.

If it seems like your growth in your Christian life isn't what you want it to be and know it should be, then this book will be like "Miracle Grow" for the seed. Apply these truths liberally, give it time and an abundant harvest awaits you.

—**Andrew Wommack**
President and Founder of Andrew Wommack Ministries and Charis Bible College

INTRODUCTION

WE had only been in Chile for a few days. After ten months in Guatemala studying Spanish, my family of five had moved to Concepción, Chile to begin to fulfill God's call to sow our lives into that beautiful land.

We had come to Chile to work with a Chilean pastor who was now taking me on a walking tour of downtown Concepción. In the main plaza of the city, we sat down on the edge of the fountain. I noticed two unusually dressed ladies standing across the plaza looking at us. I asked the pastor about them. He glanced at them and quickly responded that they were gypsies. I had never seen gypsies before, but they certainly looked like what I had seen in the movies.

The two ladies walked across the plaza and stood before us. One of them asked, "Would you like to know your future?" The pastor turned to me and indicated that they wanted to read our palms. He then turned to the two ladies and said something I will never forget. "I already know my future. Would you like to know yours?"

The two gypsy ladies looked at each other and one said to the other, "I told you he had power." At that, they walked away.

That encounter and that brief answer given by my pastor friend impacted me. I understood that he was speaking of the eternal destinies of those who are born again and those who aren't. But something else was sparked in me. I began to think about the future not just in terms of eternal destiny, but in terms of our lives on earth. Can we know the future? Can we play any part in shaping the future? Are we simply at the mercy of world events, natural disasters, and political movements?

In this book, I want to challenge you to rethink the future. You may ask, "How can I rethink something that hasn't happened yet?" But what I am suggesting is that you rethink how you approach the future. Be willing to consider that you may have more influence over your future than you ever thought. In fact, I would propose that God has given us the potential to shape our futures.

The just shall live by faith, not fate. And faith is all about the future! The author of Hebrews spoke by the Spirit about faith and how it touches the future.

> Now faith is the **substance of things hoped** for, the evidence of things not seen (Hebrews 11:1).

Hope is always about the future. Faith is the certainty of a future that cannot yet be seen with the natural eye. Is it possible to have certainty about the future? In many ways, yes. Whether we can know every circumstance or not, we can have assurance of our own purpose and destiny.

WHERE WILL YOUR FUTURE COME FROM?

Most of us give only fleeting thought to the future. You may try to imagine what is in store for your family, your job, your living situation, and your health. Normal people desire a happy, prosperous future. However, the present can be so demanding and draining that the future gets forgotten. We are often just trying to survive the here and now. Where does the future come from? Can I really shape my future and that of my family?

Jesus gave us a major revelation about where the future comes from.

> *A good man out of the good treasure of his heart* **brings forth** *good; and an evil man out of the evil treasure of his heart brings forth evil. For out of the abundance of the heart his mouth speaks* (Luke 6:45).

Anything that is "brought forth" is going to happen in the future. And according to Jesus, it can be good or evil depending on the condition of one's heart.

In every heart there exists a treasure. This treasure can consist of good or evil. Proverbs 4:23 tells us, "*Keep your heart with all diligence, for out of it spring the issues of life.*" Why is the heart so important? Your heart is the true source of your life and your future. It is the heart that decides whether we live by the Spirit (God's desires) or by the flesh (lustful desires). It is in the heart that thoughts are conceived, emotions are nurtured or ignored, and actions are born. It is the heart that can choose to see what God sees or remain focused on the perceived limitations of life. A good man or woman will bring forth his future from the treasure of his heart.

Jesus again spoke of the heart and its potential to bring forth the future.

> *For out of the heart proceed evil thoughts, murders, adulteries, fornications, thefts, false witness, blasphemies* (Matthew 15:19).

In every heart there exists a treasure.

All these evil things that Jesus spoke of haven't happened yet. They are future events and they have a source. In other words, your future resides in your heart. Your future consists of thoughts, words, and actions that have yet to be expressed. You can allow your heart to be a warehouse for the past, i.e., a storehouse of the hurts, the anger, the offenses, failures, and memories that you may choose to live from. Or it can be a factory of faith for the future. Your treasure can consist of the promises of God, your identity in Christ, a vision of success, the expectation of goodness and mercy, and the actions of kindness. In your heart reside the issues of life.

You are the developer of your future. Can your decisions, attitudes, and actions actually change your future? Absolutely. You have sovereign control over your thoughts, words, and actions. How you respond to the circumstances in this fallen world is up to you. We are going to look at the many ways we are shaping our futures and learn how God has provided for us to have abundant life.

Fill the treasure of your heart with the seed of God's Word and decide to bring forth an overcoming future.

CHAPTER 1

THE ABUNDANT FUTURE

WHEN I minister and teach, I often ask the question, "How many of you would like more?" Some will ask, "More what?" I will then respond, "More love, more joy, more peace, more health, more prosperity, more opportunities," etc. Everyone's hands go up at the prospect of having more. That is not a bad desire. In fact, it is a God thing. God is a God of more.

Consider the following declarations from God's Word.

> Now to Him who is able to do **exceedingly abundantly** above all that we ask or think, according to the power that works in us (Ephesians 3:20).

> For if by the one man's offense death reigned through the one, much more those who receive **abundance of grace** and of the gift of righteousness will reign in life through the One, Jesus Christ (Romans 5:17).

*And God is able to make all grace abound toward you, that you, always having all sufficiency in all things, may have **an abundance for every good work*** (2 Corinthians 9:8).

*He who did not spare His own Son, but delivered Him up for us all, how shall He not with Him also **freely give us all things?*** (Romans 8:32)

*Give, and it will be given to you: **good measure, pressed down, shaken together, and running over** will be put into your bosom. For with the same measure that you use, it will be measured back to you* (Luke 6:38).

*I have come that they may have life, **and that they may have it more abundantly*** (John 10:10).

These are just a few of many verses that demonstrate the goodness of God and His heart to bless His children. In each case, we find the potential future being described. Words such as "is able to do," "those who receive...will reign," "is able to make all grace abound," and "it will be given to you," all describe the possibilities of the future. Who is the prosperous future for? It is for those who release the "power that works in us," those who "receive the abundance of grace and the gift of righteousness," and those who "give." We will spend much more time on these and many other verses in order to understand the role we play in shaping the future that is possible.

It is so destructive to misunderstand the heart of God and believe that He is the one sending problems our way, allowing loss, death, and destruction in our lives and "testing" us for some mysterious purpose that we never quite figure out. The thief comes to steal, kill, and destroy (see John 10:10). *God is not the thief!* Jesus came that we might have abundant life! Sadly, many have confused the work of the enemy with the work of God.

I understand that Jesus promised His followers that there would be persecution and tribulation in this world, and I am not overlooking that reality. Those who live godly in Christ Jesus will suffer persecution (see 2 Tim. 3:12). *But even if persecution comes our way, it can't extinguish the nature of God's abundance within us.* More joy, peace, love, and favor are possible even in the midst of persecution. Even if we lose every material possession for our faith, there is more than enough of God's grace and love available to us. Abundance begins in the heart. Your future resides in your heart.

How did God intend for mankind to relate to this planet?

> *The heaven, even the heavens, are the Lord's; but the earth He has given to the children of men* (Psalm 115:16).

We need to understand that God's intention was for men and women to have dominion over His creation. When we speak of the future, we must consider how God has ordained His creation to function. The Designer of the world who sustains all things with His Word and has given the earth to man should know how we can get the maximum from life. He *is* maximum life! If the earth was to be governed by humans, then the future of both earth and humans had to have been in the heart of God from before creation.

Let's consider creation in the beginning.

> *Then God said, "Let the earth bring forth grass, the herb that yields seed, and the fruit tree that yields fruit according to its kind, **whose seed is in itself**, on the earth"; and it was so* (Genesis 1:11).

What was in God's heart? What was His plan? If we consider that the Garden of Eden was a specific place in a specific location, and that the plants and trees of the Garden carried seed, we can easily understand that God's vision for the future was to see the Garden spread across the face of the earth. What was His strategy for making this growth possible? Seeds. We are going to study the revelation contained in seeds in great detail. *Seeds carry the invisible future in the visible present.*

Paul alluded to this when he declared that God's invisible attributes can be seen through His creation.

> *For since the creation of the world **His invisible attributes are clearly seen**, being understood by the things that are made, even His eternal power and Godhead* (Romans 1:20)

Let's consider this for a moment. Since creation, the invisible things of God are clearly seen and can be understood by the things that God made. This is an incredible truth and a key to understanding the future. Seeds carry His invisible attributes.

If we were to travel back in time to the Garden of Eden, we would be able to see with our physical eyes what God made. We would see the trees, flowers, vegetables, animals, and perhaps even Adam and Eve. Before sin entered the picture, everything was perfect and programmed for the future. This is why the Scriptures tell us, *"Then God saw everything that He had made, and indeed it was very good"* (Gen. 1:31).

Every plant, tree, animal, and even Adam and Eve were all visible. But we read in Romans 1:20 that the invisible things of God are clearly seen in what has been made. There is more in the Garden than meets the eye.

If we were to continue our walk through the Garden, perhaps we would see a peach hanging from a tree. The peach looks good for food, but we still haven't seen what is on the inside. Once we take a bite from the peach, a new revelation comes to light.

> *Seeds carry the invisible future in the visible present.*

> *And God said, "See, I have given you every herb that yields seed which is on the face of all the earth,* ***and every tree whose fruit yields seed****; to you it shall be for food"* (Genesis 1:29).

In that which is seen we can begin to see the unseen. In every plant and tree that is for food, there is seed. God said that the seed yielding plants and trees would be for food. Do you see what is being said? God's plan for the future of mankind was contained in the seeds of His creation. The invisible things of God are clearly seen in what He has made. *The future that we can't see resides in the seeds that we can see!*

Every seed carries its potential future within it. Its future can be released to create unlimited growth and abundance (the attributes of God), or it can be neglected and wasted. Every seed is created to reproduce according to its kind (nature). The multiplication of seeds can go on forever. In each seed exists the potential for super abundance. But those seeds must be planted. God's heart from the beginning was for abundance and prosperity in creation. He locked that vision into the concept of a seed.

> *The future that we can't see resides in the seeds that we can see!*

Though God programmed the future into the seeds of creation, the future can only be unlocked if the seeds are planted. That is where man comes into the picture. Seeds not planted will never release their potential. Their future will be lost. Man is the one who determines which seeds impact the future and which are ignored.

What about your future? Is the future just a series of random events that you must respond to and learn to accept? Is the future something that God makes up as we go through life? Or is the future predetermined and settled, and there is nothing you can do about it? Could the future be something that holds multiple possibilities that we can shape? Is it possible we get to choose our futures? The answer is very interesting.

When we consider Adam and Eve as the first two and the only two humans on the earth (Eve was the mother of all the living; see Gen. 3:20), and we understand God's command that they "be fruitful and multiply" (Gen. 1:28), we must conclude that *all future humans were packaged into Adam and Eve*. The entire human race in all of its current diversity existed in Adam and Eve in "seed" form. No new humans have been introduced into the world apart from Adam and Eve in the beginning. And remember that He said His creation "was very good" (Gen. 1:31).

No evil, no sickness, no poverty, no tragedy, no heartache, no loss, and no death were included in that which God created. All of the future for the earth and for man was complete and was included in "that which is seen" (creation) but was "unseen" (seeds). What we focus on holds the power over our lives. If we focus on the circumstances, we will be subject to them. If we focus on the power of the seed, we can shape the future. Paul spoke of looking at things that are not seen.

> *While we do not look at the things which are seen, but at the things which are not seen. For the things which are seen are temporary, but the things which are not seen are eternal* (2 Corinthians 4:18).

The things which are not seen (the invisible things of God) can be clearly seen by what has been made. While that sounds confusing, it is the key to understanding the future and, more importantly, *your future!* That which is seen, a peach for example, carries within a seed, which carries within the potential for unlimited peach trees and peaches—for the future! Those trees and peaches are unseen at the moment, but if you can see the seed with the eyes of faith, you can see the possible future contained within.

Let's go a little deeper before we begin to put this all together. What did God have in mind for you from all eternity? Or are you just an accident? You and I were "in" Adam and Eve from the beginning. Every possible human who could ever be was "packaged" in seed form into the very visible first couple. Did God see us, know us, and have a purpose for us from the beginning? We will consider the following verse written by the apostle Paul many times in this book. Let's take our first look.

> *Who has saved us and called us with a holy calling, not according to our works, but according to **His own purpose and grace** which was given to us in Christ Jesus **before time began*** (2 Timothy 1:9).

This is an incredible verse. The "package" of humanity that was contained in Adam and Eve in seed form was given purpose and grace *before time began*. And God saw what He had created and said it was "very good!" And you were in the "package" that was very good.

What does this mean? It means that before creation and before time began, God saw every human who could ever be born and established purpose and grace for them in Christ. In other words, in the "seed" of Adam and Eve, you already existed in the heart of God and you were given purpose—and grace for that purpose! God revealed something of this in His revelation to Jeremiah.

Before I formed you in the womb I knew you; before you were born I sanctified you (Jeremiah 1:5).

For I know the thoughts that I think toward you, says the Lord, thoughts of peace and not of evil, to give you a future and a hope (Jeremiah 29:11).

While these verses are spoken toward Jeremiah and Israel in their context, the concept is much larger. God's heart for His children has not changed. The future was meant to be abundant, prosperous, and filled with grace. God knew us before our physical conception. You and I were packaged in Adam and Eve, and before sin entered the earth that "package" was very good. You were taken into consideration when God prepared the earth and gave it to mankind. *You were created for a prosperous future and a hope* (see Jer. 29:11).

I hope you will take some time to meditate on these truths. Until we can see what God intended from the beginning, we may struggle with understanding so much in our lives, and we will not fully appreciate the future that is possible.

Let me review what Scripture has revealed thus far.

Before time began, God saw each of us and infused us with purpose and grace for that purpose in Christ. He then created the world and Adam and Eve. He designed His creation with the future included. In other words, the future and all of its possibilities existed in that which was seen, but it existed in seeds. All plants, animals, and humanity in all of its potential already existed in the seeds of creation. And it was very good.

Every possible person who has ever been born or who could ever have been born was included in the heart of God and destined to have purpose and grace. Every dog breed was contained in the first dogs. Every kind of peach or apple was contained in the first peaches and apples. Every genetic variation of plant and animal brought forth by man had already been provided for by God. The infinite abundance of all living things was packaged into creation. We are simply discovering what God included as the future unfolds.

What God created was "very good." However, what we see today is often very bad. But before we consider the consequences of sin, it is important to grasp the heart of God for His creation and His grace and purpose for your life. Those things have not disappeared.

Let's go back to the Garden of Eden for a few minutes and give some more thought to what God has created.

CHAPTER 2

THE POWER
OF THE SEED

A S we have established, the invisible things of God are clearly seen by what He has made. In every living thing we find the principle of the seed, and every seed is designed to reproduce according to its kind (nature). Apple trees will produce apple trees, and elephants will produce elephants.

Man was created to reproduce himself as well.

Then God said, "Let Us make man in Our image, according to Our likeness" (Genesis 1:26).

Adam and Eve and all who were to come forth from them were created in the image of God. God's image and all of the possibilities of His attributes, nature, authority, and provision were deposited into Adam and Eve. Before we unpack this subject, let's consider it on a more basic level.

Let's imagine for a moment that I can travel in time back to the Garden of Eden. As I walk through the Garden, I come across a watermelon. From the outside (that which is visible) I can only imagine what might be inside. After opening the watermelon, I find the incredible, juicy fruit within. I love watermelon, and this watermelon that God created is delicious! As I eat the watermelon, I notice seeds. I remember when I was a boy that the seeds were in the way. But they did serve a purpose. With the vision of an eight-year-old, I purposed the seeds for spitting at my sister. That may not have been God's purpose, but that was all I could see at the time.

As I grew older, I learned that I could plant a few seeds and grow some watermelons. I remember such a project for Cub Scouts. Those same seeds were now "purposed" differently. Let's say that as I grew over the years, I began to see the potential of growing enough watermelons to take to the farmer's market. I have now purposed those same seeds for bigger things. Perhaps I would then get a bigger vision. I could buy some land and start a watermelon farm and business. I would grow enough watermelons to need employees and equipment. I could actually have a business that could supply watermelons to the whole country!

In each scenario, the seeds of the watermelon will fulfill the vision that has been assigned by the "visionary." Those seeds can be spit at a sister, planted in a small garden, or turned into an industry. The seeds don't change. They are programmed to "be fruitful and multiply." *The determining factor in the future of the seeds is the visionary!* The future of the watermelon in my kitchen is up to me. It is graced by God with unlimited potential. It has a purpose. I can either see it as food and nothing more, or I can get a vision for the future.

Humans have the same options! Every human has been infused with God's purpose and grace from before time began. The potential of God lies in each of us. But how many of us are only looking at the watermelon of life and not at the seeds?

When we look at our spouse, are we seeing the potential of God's grace or the current challenges and circumstances? When we look at our young children, are we see-ing "the terrible twos" or a mighty man or woman of God? When we look at our resources, are we seeing lack or are we seeing seeds? How we see ourselves, those around us, and our circumstances will shape our futures and the futures of others as well. We are the visionaries of the seeds we have in our lives.

The determining factor in the future of the seeds is the visionary!

Let me explain this from the life of Paul the Apostle. Before his con-version, Paul was a persecutor of the church. He was chasing down Christians and sending them to prison. It was during this rampage that Jesus spoke to him.

> *As he journeyed he came near Damascus, and suddenly a light shone around him from heaven. Then he fell to the ground, and heard a voice say-ing to him, "Saul, Saul, why are you persecuting*

*Me?" And he said, "Who are You, Lord?" Then the
Lord said, "I am Jesus, whom you are persecuting"*
(Acts 9:3-5).

In the mind of Paul (Saul), his future was to chase down
Christians and purge the land of this Christian "heresy." But
remember, God had seen Paul before time began in the per-
fection of creation, and before sin corrupted man's way on
the earth. God had something different in mind for Paul.
And it was very good. But sin had brought darkness, death,
and suffering to the planet. So God adapted His purpose for
Paul to be relevant to the need. Let's read how Paul described
it later in his ministry.

> *And I thank Christ Jesus our Lord who has enabled
> me, **because He counted me faithful**, putting me
> into the ministry, although I was formerly a blas-
> phemer, a persecutor, and an insolent man; but I
> obtained mercy because I did it ignorantly in unbe-
> lief* (1 Timothy 1:12-13).

There is a tremendous amount of revelation in these
verses. My first question is, when did Jesus count Paul faithful? When Jesus spoke to him near Damascus, Paul was
certainly not faithful. Paul even declared that he was a persecutor full of ignorance and unbelief. But Jesus counted him
faithful? What was Jesus looking at? If you can grasp this, it
could change your understanding of God and your vision for
your life.

Jesus counted Paul faithful from before time began. Paul
was included in Adam and Eve, and there was an original

purpose and grace for Paul's purpose in the heart of God. While sin in the earth had changed the circumstances, the gifts and the callings of God are unchangeable. This is why Paul would later write:

> *For the gifts and the calling of God are irrevocable* (Romans 11:29).

God saw Paul was a faithful man before Paul was born! *His zeal for persecuting the church and his ignorance and unbelief did not stop God's grace for his life.* His future was changed forever by one word from God. Paul simply had to be awakened to truth in order to begin shaping the future God had in mind for him.

Paul's future, and the future of millions over the last two thousand years, was changed because God saw what He had sown into Paul and spoke life-giving words to him. *The Gospel is God's life-giving word meant to activate the purpose and grace that were intended for you from before time began!* Will you listen?

Regardless of where you are, what you've done, or how badly you may have lived up until now, there is still a future for you. In the heart of God, that which He purposed for you from before time began is still alive in seed form. You can look at the "watermelon" of your life and get discouraged, or you can choose to see the seeds of God's grace and get a new vision. *Your future lies in the seeds of His grace that were purposed for you since creation.* Let's remember our key verse once again.

> *Who has saved us and called us with a holy calling, not according to our works, but **according to His***

own purpose and grace which was given to us in Christ Jesus before time began (2 Timothy 1:9).

You may feel it is too late to begin the future God had in mind for you. You may see yourself as damaged and on the sidelines of life. But if you are born again, on the inside of you there is a treasure! Are you willing to open it?

Watermelons can look very good on the outside or they can be marred and ugly. In spite of the outward appearance, the inside is still "bread for food and seed for the sower" (see 2 Cor. 9:10).

The potential that exists in every human has not been destroyed by sin. Each of us gets to choose what kind of future we will bring forth.

Sin has done incredible damage to the world and to humanity. People can be very damaged and can have made very bad choices. They can be suffering terrible consequences from their choices or the choices of others. They can be disillusioned, hurting, fearful, sick, and broken. But none of that has changed what God created in the beginning that was very good (see Gen. 1:31). Jesus came to bind up the broken hearted!

> *The Spirit of the Lord is upon Me, because He has anointed Me to preach the gospel to the poor; He has sent Me to heal the brokenhearted, to proclaim liberty to the captives and recovery of sight to the blind, to set at liberty those who are oppressed; to proclaim the acceptable year of the Lord* (Luke 4:18-19).

In other words, in every damaged person there are still the seeds of God's grace and purpose. Even if a watermelon falls off the truck, it still has God's potential on the inside. *There are no hopeless cases, worthless people, or impossible circumstances.* There are always the seeds of God's grace available. The future God had in mind can be harnessed and shaped. But it is up to the visionary.

When you look at your life, are you looking at the watermelon or are you "seeing" the seed? Your future depends on what you see. *You* are the visionary!

If we would choose to see the unseen, the unlimited potential that God created in the beginning, we could begin to shape our futures. We can spit the seeds of our futures, or we can plant them. Proverbs reminds us:

> *A man's stomach shall be satisfied from the fruit of his mouth; from the produce of his lips he shall be filled. Death and life are in the power of the tongue, and those who love it will eat its fruit* (Proverbs 18:20-21).

When we consider the future, we must consider how God designed the future to unfold. "Seedtime and harvest" is a natural law that is sustained by a spiritual law. All that is natural in God's creation has a spiritual reality behind it. There is a visible world and an invisible world. If God has established the power of the seed in the physical world, it is because there is a spiritual truth that sustains it in the invisible world. God declared this to Noah after the flood.

> *While the earth remains, seedtime and harvest, cold and heat, winter and summer, and day and night shall not cease* (Genesis 8:22).

This is a pretty conclusive statement. If seedtime and harvest shall not cease on the earth, then the spiritual law that sustains those realities must still be alive and active. The natural order of God's creation can only exist on the authority of God Himself. The laws of nature are a reflection of the spiritual laws that sustain them. The author of Hebrews says it this way:

> *By faith we understand that the worlds were framed by the word of God, so that the* **things which are seen were not made of things which are visible** (Hebrews 11:3).

> [Jesus] *being the brightness of His glory and the express image of His person, and* **upholding all things by the word of His power** (Hebrews 1:3).

That which is seen was created by that which was not seen to the human eye. Spiritual reality brought forth our visible, tangible reality, and Jesus upholds that which is seen by His Word. Seedtime and harvest are physical realities that are sustained by a spiritual reality. Why do I emphasize this point? If we can understand how God chose to bring increase to the earth and to humanity, then we can choose to cooperate with His will and shape our futures in a positive way. *Life consists of seedtime and harvest.*

Let's continue to consider the seed. God's infinite wisdom, His grace, and His desires can all be understood from these small packages that carry so much potential. Jesus gave us a clear understanding of how His Kingdom functions.

The kingdom of heaven is like a man who sowed good seed in his field (Matthew 13:24)

The revelation in this brief statement is tremendous. When we consider the immediate, natural implications, we can think of a farmer and his crops. But let's turn our eyes upward and think in terms of God and His plan for the earth. Think of God as the One who sowed the Garden of Eden, all flora and fauna, and man himself as the "good seed." Everything was created to reproduce after its "kind" or nature. The abundant multiplication of all things created by God was the goal.

From Genesis 1, we understand that God's vision for the earth and for man was multiplication. The future of creation was programmed into the "seeds" of the first plants, animals, and humans. As we have seen, *everything for the future was locked into the seeds of the present.*

> *The future is all around us in seed form!*

God designed infinite increase into the seed. Every seed contains a harvest, and the harvest contains more seed for future harvests. God's sovereign decision was to package the future into the seeds present at the time of creation. *Nothing new has been added by God to the original creation.* Everything for abundance, multiplication, and the future was all programmed into the earth and into mankind in the beginning.

Returning to Matthew 13:24, *"The kingdom of heaven is like a man who sowed good seed in his field,"* we begin to understand that concept of the future from God's perspective. *The future is all around us in seed form!* The future is in our hearts, our minds, our words, our actions, and our attitudes. We have been entrusted with the future by the Creator, but we must understand the package in which it comes—*seeds!*

Every thought, word, action, attitude, and resource can be the seed of blessing or destruction. Those seeds shape our future. In fact, we are all shaping our futures whether we know it or not.

Some thoughts about seeds:

- A seed is a small package programmed to produce limitless harvests.

- A seed is as small as it will ever be. Its possible future will always be great.

- A seed cannot deny its nature. It cannot lie. It will reproduce according to its nature.

- A seed must be planted in order for its future to be unlocked.

- Every seed is a potential door from the present into the future.

- Every harvest requires a seed.

- Your future is contained in the seeds you have in your life right now.

CHAPTER 3

WHAT IS THE FUTURE?

Never make predictions, especially about the future.

—Casey Stengel

THE famous baseball personality, Casey Stengel, may have been going for a laugh with that statement, but it captures the thinking of most of us. We tend to regard the future with a variety of emotions based upon our outlook on life. When the subject of the future comes up, some are ambivalent, others fearful, others depressed, and others enthusiastic. Very few actually stop to consider that today's decisions will influence tomorrow's possibilities.

When we think about the future, we can break it down into four components. The future consists of thoughts we haven't thought yet, words we haven't spoken yet, actions we haven't done yet, and circumstances that we don't know of yet.

Billions of people on the earth have the capacity to think new thoughts, say new words, and do new things. All of these thoughts, words, and actions create circumstances that can impact a few people, or nations, or even the entire world. Apart from the uncertainty of fallen nature itself, all other circumstances are manmade.

Let's consider the four components of the future on a more personal level.

THE SEEDS OF THOUGHTS

Your thoughts are yours alone. They are seeds that carry the potential of the future. We each have control over what we think and how we think. Those who spend their time daydreaming, thinking foolish things, or planning ways to satisfy their carnal desires are impacting their futures whether they know it or not. Those who focus their minds on opportunities or ideas about how to bless others are also impacting their futures. In the days of Noah, the thoughts of fallen men were quite destructive.

> *And God saw that the wickedness of man was great in the earth, and that **every imagination of the thoughts of his heart was only evil continually*** (Genesis 6:5 KJV).

If you are familiar with the story of the flood in Genesis, you will notice how the thoughts of men before the flood impacted their future. Collectively, men had given themselves over to the lusts of their flesh. Their thinking played a part in their destiny. This truth is seen throughout the Scriptures. Lost men's thoughts create the environment for destruction. They determine their future. What about the thoughts of those who are in tune with God?

> *The thoughts of the diligent tend only to plenteousness* (Proverbs 21:5 KJV).

Notice how the thoughts of the diligent bring forth abundance. *Thoughts do that!* The New King James Version says, *"The plans of the diligent lead surely to plenty."* A plan is a thought. How we think can determine our futures. The mind that is renewed to God's Word and God's promises will think in ways that will unlock the blessings of God. In other words, our futures are impacted and shaped by our thoughts. One of the most powerful truths in Scripture concerns the thoughts of our hearts.

> *For as he thinks in his heart, so is he* (Proverbs 23:7).

While this statement is found in a specific context, like many such statements in Scripture it reveals a "concept" that far exceeds the context. How we think in our hearts determines how we will speak and act. Our present is a reflection of how we have thought in the past. The way we have thought about God, about ourselves, about those around us, and about our circumstances has in large part produced who we are today. Those who live in fear think fearful thoughts. Those who are offended nurse those offenses. Others have dreamed big dreams and believed that the sky is the limit. In every case we find ourselves, at this moment in time, having been shaped by our thoughts.

If the present is a reflection of the past, then the future will be a reflection of the present. The thoughts we are thinking today are planting the seeds for our futures. Paul said:

> *Finally, brethren, whatever things are true, whatever things are noble, whatever things are just, whatever things are pure, whatever things are lovely, whatever things are of good report, if there is any virtue and if there is anything praiseworthy— meditate on these things* (Philippians 4:8).

Can you imagine a mind filled only with pure thoughts? Don't you think that thinking thoughts of truth and things that are noble might impact your future? Paul spoke to this again in the book of Romans.

> *And do not be conformed to this world, but be transformed by the renewing of your mind, **that you may prove what is that good and acceptable and perfect will of God*** (Romans 12:2).

In this well-known passage, we see that it is possible to be conformed to this world, i.e., the world's way of doing things. Those who are conformed to this world will have a future that reflects the limitations that the world imposes. Only a mind renewed to God's thoughts will know what the perfect will of God is. And the will of God is always pointed toward a prosperous future and abundant life.

Our minds contain powerful potential. How we think and meditate can create incredible opportunities or can create insurmountable barriers. The greatest minds in the world feed on solving problems, thinking beyond the known, and looking for answers for the unknown. Sadly, many others fill their minds with fearful thoughts of doubt and despair. Both kinds of people are shaping their futures. Have you ever wondered how God thinks?

> *"For My thoughts are not your thoughts, nor are your ways My ways," says the Lord* (Isaiah 55:8).

From this verse we can understand that there are two kinds of thinking available to us. There is worldly, natural thinking, and there is the God kind of thinking. What does worldly, natural thinking look like? Let's consider the story of the children of Israel sending spies into the Promised Land.

> *And the Lord spoke to Moses, saying, "Send men to spy out the land of Canaan,* **which I am giving to the children of Israel**; *from each tribe of their fathers you shall send a man, every one a leader among them"* (Numbers 13:1-2).

Immediately, we notice that the Lord had already decided to give the land of Canaan to Israel. This was not an excursion to see whether or not the land could be theirs. *It was an expedition to discover that which God had already given.* The twelve spies were each leaders among the people. They weren't unmotivated men. Let's see how they spoke upon returning from their mission.

> *"We went to the land where you sent us. It truly flows with milk and honey, and this is its fruit. Nevertheless* **the people who dwell in the land are strong; the cities are fortified and very large...We are not able** *to go up against the people, for they are stronger than we." And they gave the children of Israel a bad report of the land which they had spied out, saying, "The land through which we have gone as spies is* **a land that devours its inhabitants,** *and all the people whom we saw in it are men of great stature. There we saw the giants (the descendants of Anak came from the giants); and* **we were like grasshoppers in our own sight,** *and so we were in their sight"* (Numbers 13:27-28,31-33).

The leaders of the people had wrong thinking about themselves. They saw themselves as grasshoppers, a people that could easily be conquered by the giants of the land. They also had wrong thinking about the circumstances. They saw the strong and fortified cities and decided that they were unable to do anything about it. Finally, they had wrong thinking about God.

> **Why has the Lord brought us to this land to fall by the sword,** *that our wives and children should become victims? Would it not be better for us to return to Egypt?* (Numbers 14:3)

Remember that God had already declared that He had given them the land. Nevertheless, they now accused God of wanting them to die by the sword. Can you see the pattern of wrong thinking here? They didn't see themselves as God saw them. Thus, they imagined the circumstances to be far beyond their ability to overcome. Finally, they blamed God. *The seeds of the future were being sown by wrong thinking.*

As we know, the outcome wasn't good. The children of Israel had shaped their future based upon the fearful thinking and speaking of 10 of the 12 spies. Their fear would subjugate them to 40 years in the wilderness until that generation of fearful men died off. This was not the future God had in mind for Israel.

How often have we thwarted God's purpose for our lives with our fearful thinking? God's thoughts toward us are forever positive and life giving. But we can be conformed to this world and short circuit God's intentions with our fearful, worldly thoughts.

> *For I know the thoughts that I think toward you, says the Lord, thoughts of peace and not of evil, to give you a future and a hope* (Jeremiah 29:11).

God is also thinking, but His thoughts are positive and life giving. The "future and a hope" in Jeremiah 29:11 is God's heart for your future. As men created in His image, we can ignore God's vision and His thoughts and establish our own. Israel created a future of wandering in the wilderness for 40 years because of wrong thinking, in spite of God's desire for them.

Thought seeds followed by word seeds shaped the future of Israel for 40 years.

WRONG THINKING ABOUT GOD

Wrong thinking about God has done untold damage to the body of Christ. Blaming God or attributing calamity to God has derailed the future of many. Whole theologies have been established to explain that God allows tragedies, sends tragedies, or uses tragedies to teach us something. Religious phrases are repeated frequently that deflect the blame for all things to God. Phrases such as "God allowed it," or "Everything happens for a reason" have done much to paralyze Christians in their faith. In fact, many do not even know what it means to live by faith. They have been programmed to live by fate and call it faith. Their futures are being shaped by a spirit of fatalism and resignation. Their futures are being shaped by wrong thinking about God.

I recently came across a saying that sounded quite pious but actually was entirely wrong: "Sometimes God will put you in a battle empty-handed so that when you do get the victory you will know it wasn't you, but Him" (author unknown).

Such a saying is looking to the future but through a very warped lens. The first unfortunate concept is that God will put us in a battle. Second, He will do so and give us nothing with which to fight. Third, He wants us to be victorious without doing anything.

So much of our modern Christian theology is founded on wrong conclusions about the nature of God, the nature of man, and man's purpose in the earth. Practically everything in the above quote is wrong on every count. The result of such an approach to life is that we become shaped by circumstances rather than actively participating in shaping them. Wrong thinking can sink your future!

Let's look at the elements of the above statement. What does it mean that "God puts us in battles"? The idea is that God is manipulating us, pulling strings as if we were puppets and creating circumstances that we can't escape as a part of some celestial plan. In the light of the New Covenant and the finished work of the cross, can this be true? God doesn't put us in battles. Battles (I assume this is referring to trials, tribulations, temptations, and perhaps even sickness or economic distress) are a part of the fallen world in which we live. God doesn't send hard times our way to teach us anything. He sent the Word to teach and perfect us. Remember, God's creation, purpose, and grace for mankind was established before time began, and once completed it was "very good" (see Gen. 1:31 and 2 Tim. 1:9).

Does God put us in battles, or has God's grace equipped us for the battles that exist in this fallen world? Paul wrote to Timothy:

> *All Scripture is given by inspiration of God, and is profitable for doctrine, for reproof, for correction, for instruction in righteousness, that the man of God may be complete, thoroughly equipped for every good work* (2 Timothy 3:16-17).

Please notice that it is the Word of God that reproves and corrects that we might be thoroughly equipped in life. The tests and trials of life are not our teachers. *If sickness, loss, and hard times are our teachers, we are in the wrong kingdom!*

While it is certainly possible to learn from hard times, we don't have to go through them to be complete. God is not sending hard times and is not leading you into them. Trials and temptations are not from God.

> *If sickness, loss, and hard times are our teachers, we are in the wrong kingdom!*

While I have been in hard times of distress and confusion, I have never once believed that God was the author of my distress. My renewed thinking has created a door of deliverance. I know that God is for me, not against me, so I quickly understand that I have missed it somewhere or I have run into some resistance from the enemy. Such an approach impacts my future for success. With confidence I can approach the challenge knowing that God desires my victory, not my suffering. Those who believe that God is creating hard times to "test" them have unknowingly shaped their futures for more hard times. James declares emphatically:

Let no one say when he is tempted, "I am tempted by God"; for God cannot be tempted by evil, nor does He Himself tempt anyone. But each one is tempted when he is drawn away by his own desires and enticed. Then, when desire has conceived, it gives birth to sin; and sin, when it is full-grown, brings forth death. Do not be deceived, my beloved brethren. Every good gift and every perfect gift is from above, and comes down from the Father of lights, with whom there is no variation or shadow of turning (James 1:13-17).

It is interesting that the Greek word for *tempt* is defined by the word *test* in Strong's Concordance. The passage in James could just as easily read that God does not "test" anyone. The context is dealing with being tempted or tested with evil, and the conclusion is that evil is not from God. Only good gifts come from Him.

If we are going to be effective in shaping our futures, we must be clear as to the source of anything that would come to steal, kill, or destroy (see John 10:10). So much of the future depends on this understanding.

Let's move on to the next portion of the quote: "Sometimes God will put you in a battle empty-handed." Empty-handed? We are never empty-handed! Seeing ourselves as empty-handed is a major blow to the truth of our inheritance in Christ. It is an attitude that approaches the future as a victim and not as a victor. Are we empty-handed in our Christian walk? We have been given the Name of Jesus, the better covenant, better promises, the blood of Jesus, the Holy Spirit, the armor of God, the Word of God, the faith of God, the keys of the Kingdom, authority to tread upon all the work of the enemy, the gifts of the Spirit, and we are one spirit with Him! We are seated with Him in heavenly places! We are more than conquerors! How could we ever see ourselves as empty-handed? This thinking comes from the "sovereign God" mentality that believes that God controls all things and we are mere puppets in His play.

Being empty-handed describes someone who has no influence over their future. The reality is that as believers we have been equipped to enforce the will of God within our sphere of influence and shape the future according to His will.

Let's continue analyzing this quote: "Sometimes God will put you in a battle empty-handed so that when you do get the victory you will know it wasn't you, but Him."

To begin with, we aren't trying to "get the victory"! We are called to enforce the victory that was won on the cross! As long as we think we are trying to win a victory, we will never enter into the victory that was already won. As born-again Christians, we start from a place of victory! Jesus already sat down at the right hand of God and has given to His church the victory over the enemy. It is now up to us to enforce what has been given.

The quote continues: "you will know it wasn't you, but Him." The last point of the quote is more subtle but equally important. Though the victory over darkness was certainly because of Him, our role as enforcers is entirely up to us. When we establish God's will in our lives and the lives of others, it *is* because of us. We can change our futures and the futures of others! Paul described this truth in one of my favorite verses.

> *Now to Him who is able to do exceedingly abundantly above all that we ask or think, **according to the power that works in us*** (Ephesians 3:20).

The power to receive from God more than we can ask or think works in us! God's will for our continual victory remains in our hands. We can live by faith or live by fate. We truly need to recognize and walk in the "power that works in us." The quote we have been discussing has more to do with fate than faith.

So many well-meaning Christians are being stripped of their capacity to reign in life because of the fatalism of the theology expressed in the quote. Rather than enforcing Christ's victory and shaping our futures, we are being told to just sit back and "let God do it." What does that even mean?

God didn't tell Adam and Eve to just sit back and let Him run the Garden. He told them to *"dress it and to keep it"* (Gen. 2:15 KJV). He gave them every tree and plant bearing seed after its own kind. In those seeds existed the heart of God for their future. Adam and Eve were to use the seeds to extend the Garden of Eden over the face of the earth. The Garden was conceived in the heart of God but delegated to Adam and Eve. It was their responsibility.

Man was created in the image of God in order to reflect God's nature and do God's works on the earth. It has never been about God doing everything while we sit back and watch. We have the capacity to see the future with spiritual eyes and bring it forth with the seeds we have on hand. The visionary determines the extent of the possibilities. What we see and how we choose to see it shapes our futures and the futures of others. Remember that Paul said:

> *While we look not at the things which are seen, but at the things which are not seen: for the things which are seen are temporal; but the things which are not seen are eternal* (2 Corinthians 4:18 KJV).

Wrong thinking about God is perhaps the greatest cause for the rejection of the gospel. Millions want nothing to do with God because Christians have described Him as controlling, mysterious, vengeful, and unpredictable. Who wants to serve a God who wipes out regions with earthquakes and hurricanes? Who would be drawn to a God who "allows" sex trafficking and child abuse? What benefit is there in serving a God who wants us to sit back and just let things happen?

Instead of understanding man's role in God's creation, many have decided to look the other way. Rather than shaping the future, most are resigned to take whatever comes and quote religious sayings about how it will all be OK in the end.

Our thoughts about God are shaping our futures. Wrong thinking can be fatal!

THE SEEDS OF WORDS

Once we understand the power of thought, we must move to the most powerful force that God has given man—the power of words!

"You will never amount to anything!" How many of us heard these words as children? They were probably spoken in a moment of frustration by our parents or other adults, but even frustrated words carry power. These words sow images into our hearts. These words can curse our futures until they are purged by the more powerful Word of God.

Adam and Eve were created in the image of God and, unlike the animals, they were endued with the capacity to speak, to reason, and to express whatever resides in the treasure of the heart. Man is the pinnacle of God's creation, and the power of words that God used to create all things now resides within the man He created. Man's future in Eden would soon be impacted by words—both words that were heard and words that were spoken.

As we consider how we shape our futures, we must understand the power of choice that God has given to us. By His Word He created and sustains the earth and all that is in it. By His Word He created Adam and Eve and placed them in Eden. By His Word He gave them authority over His creation.

> *The heaven, even the heavens, are the Lord's; but* **the earth He has given to the children of men** (Psalm 115:16).

And again:

> *What is man that You are mindful of him, and the son of man that You visit him? For You have made him a little lower than the angels, and You have crowned him with glory and honor.* **You have made him to have dominion over the works of Your hands; You have put all things under his feet** (Psalm 8:4-6).

This truth is not understood by many sincere believers. If you don't believe you have been equipped and given authority, you will never step out and exert that authority. You will allow life to overwhelm you and be resigned to your fate. Religion will then convince you that fatalism is actually faith. Rather than being God's ambassadors of His Kingdom, bringing light, life, and healing to a hurting world, many have become victims of religious fatalism.

Let's return to the Garden and follow the story of Adam and Eve. God gave the earth to Adam and Eve and by extension to those who would be born to them. By His Word He allowed them to eat of every tree of the Garden except one—the Tree of the Knowledge of Good and Evil. God warned Adam of the consequence of rebellion. Adam was programmed for a future of paradise and peace. It was all within his grasp. It was God's will and purpose for him. However, a new "speaker" arrived on the scene. Words are powerful and words were about to change man's destiny.

The serpent came with new words. It is important to remember that nothing had changed in God's creation. All of the goodness that God had created and all of the desires of His heart remained unchanged. However, competing words were spoken by the serpent.

> *Then the serpent said to the woman, "You will not surely die. For God knows that in the day you eat of it your eyes will be opened, and you will be like God, knowing good and evil"* (Genesis 3:4-5).

The future now hung in the balance. God's original words could be believed and declared, or the serpent's "fake news" could be believed and acted on. The destiny of mankind was at stake. God did not step in to stop the drama. He had given the earth to man, and man had a right to choose his future. You and I have the same right!

Adam and Eve's choice to listen to the words of the serpent and ignore the words of God changed history, changed the planet, and changed the spiritual force that would influence the earth from that time forward. The serpent became "the god of this age." Once his words were believed and God's words were rejected, the spiritual environment of the planet and of the future was dramatically changed. Notice how Paul described the outcome of Adam's sin with regard to the serpent.

> *But even if our gospel is veiled, it is veiled to those who are perishing, whose minds **the god of this age** has blinded, who do not believe, lest the light of the gospel of the glory of Christ, who is the image of God, should shine on them* (2 Corinthians 4:3-4).

The words of the serpent could not create the future, but if his words were believed, they could cause Adam and Eve to change the future and lose what God had intended. Sadly, we know the outcome. The serpent became the "god of this age." He became the spiritual influence that has trapped mankind in ignorance, fear, and corruption. What we believe and what we say are powerful influences on our futures.

As we consider the power of words in the light of our previous discussion of the seed, it is easy to see that words are seeds. Jesus referred to God's Word as seed.

> *Now the parable is this: The seed is the word of God* (Luke 8:11).

Our own words are a fruit that springs from the heart.

> *A man's stomach shall be satisfied from the fruit of his mouth; from the produce of his lips he shall be filled* (Proverbs 18:20).

In the fruit of our mouths there is seed. That is how God designed creation. In other words, the produce of our lips carries the seeds that bear the nature of those words, and those words bear the nature of our hearts. Our words are seeds that have the power to reproduce according to their kind. And seeds carry the future! Remember the ten spies we discussed earlier? Their thoughts of their inability to take the Promised Land were converted into words of fear and doubt. Those word seeds were received by the children of Israel and the future was changed.

> *Words have no power until they are believed!*

So much of our future is directly related to the words we have spoken or the words that we have received, believed, and acted upon. The serpent's words were lying seeds meant to seduce and destroy. *They had no power until they were believed.*

God's words carry His nature and are designed to fulfill their purpose for the future. But their power in our lives depends upon whether or not we believe them. God's words are programmed for success and prosperity, but this will only happen in the lives of those who believe them. *Faith is simply the soil of the heart receiving and believing the seeds of God's Word.* God's Word cannot lie. It cannot change its nature. It must accomplish its purpose. But the necessary environment for the seed of the Word must be found. It is the human heart. Your future and God's purposes for you are depending on how your heart responds to God's Word.

> *So shall My word be that goes forth from My mouth; it shall not return to Me void, but it shall accomplish what I please, and it shall prosper in the thing for which I sent it* (Isaiah 55:11).

God has programmed His words to accomplish His purposes. The fact that they "prosper" speaks to the principle of multiplication found in every seed.

The future is contained in word seeds. How much of human history has been changed by words? Wars have been started, great crimes committed, marriages ruined, and destinies altered due to words. Words carry the power to influence the future and always reflect the nature of their source. A heart of bitterness and strife will release words that carry the same. And the harvest is always greater than the seed that conceived it.

Words can also be used to encourage, to lift up, to heal, and to bless. Lives can be changed by words. Love can be expressed, faith released, and hearts motivated to believe God. The power of words cannot be overestimated, which is why Jesus said, "*For out of the abundance of the heart the mouth speaks*" (Matt. 12:34). The words that come from our hearts carry the nature of our hearts. Are we speaking from a good treasure or an evil treasure?

> *A good man out of the good treasure of his heart brings forth good things, and an evil man out of the evil treasure brings forth evil things* (Matthew 12:35).

Words are seeds that have a source. The source is the heart. The condition of the heart determines the life or death packaged within the words. They will reproduce according to their kind. They carry the future.

How many of us can look back and remember hurtful, damaging words that were spoken to us or over us? How many times have we agreed with those words and decided that the declarations of others must be true? Will I never amount to anything? Will I always be poor? Will no one ever love me? When our hearts receive words of defeat, those seeds begin to grow and shape the vision we have of ourselves. Our thoughts change and our words change until we have finally conformed to the image that was spoken over us. Words have changed our future.

Returning to Matthew 12:35, Jesus said that a good man will "bring forth good things." To "bring forth" speaks of the future. Your future is in your heart. It is shaped by how you think, what you believe, and what you speak. The writer of Proverbs says this as clearly as possible.

> *Death and life are in the power of the tongue, and*
> *those who love it will eat its fruit* (Proverbs 18:21).

Both death and life are future possibilities. They are the harvest of the thoughts we think, the words we speak, and the choices we make. The words we speak are shaping our futures.

How often do we limit our own futures by speaking words of doubt? "It would be nice to have a vacation, but I don't think we can afford it this year." In that statement we find thoughts that have been looking at the watermelon, not the seeds, and declaring the future. I understand the realities of a budget, but the power to shape a future vacation was voided by negative thoughts and words. Limitations were accepted and enforced by words that bear the nature of their source—the unbelieving heart. Jesus said that His words are Spirit and life.

> *It is the Spirit who gives life; the flesh profits nothing. The words that I speak to you are spirit, and they are life* (John 6:63).

As I have said, words carry the nature of their source. Jesus's words are Spirit and life because their source (God the Father) is Spirit and life. Jesus's words carry the nature, purpose, and authority of God. Ours can as well!

THE SEEDS OF ACTIONS

Two farmers were each given two plots of fertile land, two houses to live in, barns, farm equipment, and plenty of seed. One farmer got a vision for the future and set about to bring forth a harvest. He plowed his fields and planted his seeds. The other farmer decided that if God was good enough to give him so much, He would somehow see to his future harvest and prosperity as well. He left his seed in the barn.

A couple of years passed, and the first farmer was prospering. His fields were overflowing with abundance and there was prosperity everywhere he looked. The other farmer had become bitter and poor. He was offended at the first farmer's success and wondered why God loved the other farmer more than He loved him.

Can you see the problem? Our future is not only about all that we have been given by God's grace, but also what we choose to do with what we have been given. We all begin our lives in Christ forgiven, justified, born again, a part of the family of God, filled with His Spirit, and blessed with His promises. What we do with this inheritance is up to us. We can be passive and fatalistic, or we can understand how God's Kingdom works and begin to sow from all we have received in Christ.

As we consider the future and the potential we have, we must now discuss the things we do. Like thoughts and words, our actions are seeds. Being kind to someone is a seed and cutting off someone in traffic is a seed (and a fruit!). Actions spring from the same source as words and thoughts. Jesus said it clearly:

> *For from within, out of the heart of men, proceed evil thoughts, adulteries, fornications, murders, thefts, covetousness, wickedness, deceit, lewdness, an evil eye, blasphemy, pride, foolishness. All these evil things come from within and defile a man* (Mark 7:21-23).

Out of the heart not only proceed evil thoughts, but all the actions that often follow such thoughts. Once again, your future resides in your heart.

A wise man once said, "Your body can't go anywhere that your mind hasn't gone already." In other words, actions are a fruit of what you have allowed yourself to think about. Actions are directly or indirectly related to our thoughts and words. Actions are not only the fruit of seed thoughts and seed words, they also carry their own seeds of life or destruction. They bear the nature of their source. The lazy farmer had everything the active farmer had, but his vision left him stagnant and eventually bitter.

Actions of selfishness, anger, or revenge are destroying the present and sowing more destruction for the future. People won't always know what you are thinking, but they will never forget what you did. Actions are both fruit and seed, and they impact our futures and the futures of others.

A man who thinks about going to a bar may then talk to others about accompanying him to a bar. The words have given more power to the thoughts. Finally, it is agreed that they will drive to the bar. The body can't go where the mind hasn't gone already. Upon leaving the bar, the man is intoxicated but chooses to drive anyway. During the drive he hits and kills a pedestrian. Now, futures have been forever changed. The pedestrian is dead. His future on this earth is over. All of the potential and the purpose of God for his life has been cut short. The future of the driver now includes time in prison. Not only his future but that of his family is forever impacted. The ripple effect can't be fully known. The seed of a thought has now harvested multiple changed destinies.

Actions have a powerful influence on the future. Actions are a reflection of thoughts and words. Futures are being shaped and even the lives of others will be impacted by the actions we choose. How much of your present is the harvest of your actions or the actions of others from the past? Perhaps it is time to become more involved in building a positive future.

CHAPTER 4

VISION SEEDS

C AN you see the future? Most would say "no." We tend to live our lives with our sight focused on the present and perhaps a few days ahead. If we think about the future at all, it is usually to hope that everything works out well or hope that nothing bad will happen to us. We might be actually contemplating possible harvests of past negative seeds sown and hoping those harvests don't come in.

If we become afflicted with a sickness or some other challenge comes our way, we become very focused on the present, and the future is seen with dread. Will we make it past this storm of life?

There is a verse in Hebrews that has given me a key to overcoming obstacles and having peace in the midst of the challenges of life. The verse is speaking of Moses. Moses had been born into the nation of Israel, slaves of Egypt. Through a series of divine circumstances, Moses ended up being raised in the house of the Egyptian Pharaoh as one of his sons. Moses knew of his lineage, became offended at the Egyptian treatment of the Israeli slaves, and killed an Egyptian who was mistreating one of the slaves. As a result, the Pharaoh sought to kill Moses, and Moses had to flee Egypt.

> *By faith he forsook Egypt, not fearing the wrath of the king;* **for he endured as seeing Him who is invisible** (Hebrews 11:27).

Because of the threat of death, Moses fled the comforts of Egypt. The interesting aspect of his flight is that he endured by seeing Him who is invisible! What does that mean? Moses was able to shape his future by not fearing the wrath of the king and simultaneously "seeing Him who is invisible."

Moses endured his ordeal of leaving Egypt and living in the wilderness by seeing the unseen. His spiritual sense was aware of Him who is invisible. Moses's future did not lie in Egypt. His future was in the heart of God. It was invisible to the natural eye, but very visible to the spiritual eye.

We have two sets of eyes, or two kinds of vision. Our natural eyes see only what is visible, but our spiritual eyes can see into the world of the Spirit. Seeing the invisible is the key to overcoming the visible! Moses endured by seeing God who is invisible. This set the stage for a future that would change the course of history for Israel.

God's plan for the Garden of Eden was invisible to the natural eyes of Adam and Eve but was fully packaged and ready to be activated through the unseen seeds that God designed into all living things. The future was in the seeds. The seeds contained that which could not be seen.

One man's vision can be the seed for the future of many. God's vision for His children has been written in His Word, and those who "see" it experience transformed lives.

> *Write the vision and make it plain on tablets, that he may run who reads it* (Habakkuk 2:2).

What our spirits can see (the vision) is the substance from which we can shape our lives. In the beginning, God spoke forth the universe, the planet, and all the plant and animal life. The incredible variety of plant and animal life around the world existed in the heart of God as a vision. So did man. God's vision was spoken forth and became a tangible reality. God's vision of a family was contained in Adam and Eve in seed form.

We are created in the image of God with the capacity to fellowship with Him and reproduce His desire in the earth, so we have the capacity to "see" with our spiritual eyes what God's will is. "Seeing" is the key to our futures, and seeing is birthed by "hearing."

As a young Christian in Bible college, God put into me a heart for Latin America. God can put people or places into your heart as He did for Titus, Paul's associate.

> *But thanks be to **God who puts the same earnest care for you into the heart of Titus*** (2 Corinthians 8:16).

But even though God puts something in your heart, it must be accepted, nurtured, prayed over, and acted upon. It is a *possible* future, not a predestined one. That "earnest care" in my heart for Latin America led to one false start, followed by 11 years of waiting, and finally being sent to Latin America as missionaries for over 12 years. The seed of the vision turned into a harvest of changed lives, but it took time. For 11 years, I held on to the vision, keeping myself and my growing family in a position of being ready when the door of opportunity opened. I could say that I *"endured as seeing"* something that was invisible (Heb. 11:27). By faith and patience, the seed of a vision became a harvest, but that future depended on my decision to keep the vision alive within.

Let's look at the sequence of how we can shape our futures.

So then faith comes by hearing, and hearing by the word of God (Romans 10:17).

When the spirit of man hears the Spirit of God's Word, faith is activated.

Now faith is the substance of things hoped for, the evidence of things not seen (Hebrews 11:1).

Faith is the spiritual evidence that what has been heard will be seen with our natural eyes. Faith will not doubt the Word of God and will conceive an image on the inside of us that will shape thoughts, words, and actions.

But if we hope for what we do not see, we eagerly wait for it with perseverance (Romans 8:25).

Faith is the substance of things hoped for. When we hope, it is always pointed toward something that we cannot yet see with our natural eyes, *but faith can see it with spiritual eyes.*

Faith is the evidence of things not yet seen tangibly but seen through the eyes of hope.

Let me illustrate it this way. My wife loves gardening and growing flowers. She has ordered packets of seeds over the internet, and the seeds arrive at the door. If I were to open a packet and poor the tiny seeds into my hand, I would have no idea what they are or the potential they hold. Those seeds can be traced back to the Garden of Eden when God said, "Let the earth bring forth." That is incredible but true. But to me, God's purpose in those seeds is a mystery *unless I have a picture!* The picture on the packet gives me a vision of the potential inside the packet.

A promise from God is not a new thing. It is what was packaged into creation from the beginning. *A promise from God is a picture of God's original intent for mankind!*

The promises of God are vision seeds. Vision seeds are the "pictures" God has made available to us in order to move us toward His desires for our lives. The promises of God are the pictures of His desires for your life. The realities of redemption such as healing, restoration, and provision can be vision seeds. Anything that we allow to be conceived in our hearts that reflects the nature and purpose of God can be a seed for our future.

> *A promise from God is a picture of God's original intent for mankind!*

The challenge is to have a heart that is sensitive to the vision seeds of God. Everything is competing for our vision, and the world is offering many of its own visions in an effort to steal what God has promised. Many are focused on visions of stress, fear, lack of finances, health challenges, relationship issues, broken families, politics, etc. and are so consumed with these visions that God's vision has no room in which to grow. We all have vision seeds. We are all contemplating the future on some level. The question is, who is doing the planting—God's promises or the world?

When we read of our identity in Christ, do we see it? When we read of healing, do we believe it? Does it take shape on the inside? Only that which we can "see" on the inside will find expression in our physical lives. If you see sickness, poverty, and suffering, those vision seeds will shape your thoughts, words, and actions. You will cooperate and expect what you "see."

You may not even have conscious visions of hard times. You may simply have a general expectation of a hard life. Nevertheless, it is a vision seed that will produce according to its nature.

While living in Chile as missionaries, my son decided he had outgrown his bed and desired to put his mattress on the floor. The bedframe was wood and had wooden slats to support the mattress. My wife asked me to get rid of the bedframe. As I contemplated the best way to be rid of the unneeded frame, I got a "vision."

When I was a boy, my father had built an outdoor bird cage for the purpose of raising parakeets. We had a very successful result, and that time in my life was a good memory. While looking at the bedframe, I instantly "saw" a birdcage. Someone else would have seen junk. Someone may have seen a bookshelf, or some other purpose for the wood. I saw a birdcage.

What we do with God's grace (His provision for our lives) is up to us. We are the visionaries of all that God has made available to us.

I proceeded to take apart the bed frame and build a birdcage. It was six feet tall, six feet long, two feet wide, had wheels and different doors and features. It was great! I painted it, added bird nest boxes, and bought four parakeets. As God had purposed, they were fruitful and multiplied!

Upon finishing the cage, my wife said something to me that I will never forget. I'm not quite sure how she meant it, but she said, "I didn't know you had it in you." That was a profound statement. The birdcage was "in me" based upon the raw material I had on hand. But I had to "see" a birdcage and build it. It was my vision that turned the "grace" of lumber into a birdcage, which then became the home for the future birds that were possible, but which would have never come to be without the home that I had built. The vision I had for some wood unleashed the future for some parakeets!

Jesus operated in a similar way in His earthly ministry.

> *Then Jesus answered and said to them, "Most assuredly, I say to you, the Son can do nothing of Himself, but what He sees the Father do; for whatever He does, the Son also does in like manner"* (John 5:19).

The ministry of Jesus was an outflow of what He saw the Father doing. *Jesus ministered according to a vision.* Jesus spent enough time in fellowship with the Father that vision seeds were sown into His heart for His upcoming ministry. Jesus wasn't "making it up as He went." He was living out a vision that came from the Father.

With that in mind, let us move more deeply into the subject of faith.

> *Now faith is the substance of things hoped for, the* **evidence of things not seen** (Hebrews 11:1).

Faith only deals with the unseen seeds that carry the future. We don't need faith for what we see, but for what we can't see with our natural eyes. The natural eye will see seeds as distractions (especially when eating an old fashioned watermelon), but the spiritual eye will see a possible future.

Faith is all about the potential in the seeds that God has given us. His seeds are called promises. Just as all watermelon seeds are programmed to grow when planted in the right environment, all of the promises of God are "yes" and "amen." They are all programmed to fulfill themselves.

> *For all the promises of God in Him are Yes, and in Him Amen,* **to the glory of God through us** (2 Corinthians 1:20).

Remembering our previous discussion about creation and the heart of God, His purpose and grace, and how everything He created was very good, let us consider the concept of a promise.

Is a promise a new thing that God just thought up? I don't think so. Let's look at one promise for a moment.

If any of you lacks wisdom, let him ask of God, who gives to all liberally and without reproach, and it will be given to him (James 1:5).

As we look at this promise, let's consider some implications. Why would anyone lack wisdom? Was that God's intention in creation? Or was wisdom lost in the fall of man? Wouldn't all of God's wisdom have been available to Adam and Eve as they walked and talked with Him in the Garden? Wouldn't the wisdom of God have been programmed into the original creation, being seen by the things that were made?

*For since the creation of the world His **invisible** attributes are clearly seen, being understood by the things that are made, even His eternal power and Godhead* (Romans 1:20).

God's wisdom (one of His attributes) could be understood by the things that He made. Wisdom isn't a new thing. Wisdom was lost to men through sin but is available through the "seed" of the Word. The promise of wisdom in the letter of James doesn't introduce something new into creation. It is simply a picture of God's original intention for man.

God's promises may take into account the destructive nature of sin in the earth and there may be a context involved in the promise, but the nature of the promise is a picture of God's heart from the beginning. It is a picture of a possible future! But like a packet of seeds, the picture isn't the prize. The picture is just the vision of the possibility. The seeds must be sown in order to see God's intentions fulfilled.

All of God's promises (let's call them "seeds for the future") are waiting for us to accomplish their purpose!

> For all the promises of God in Him are Yes, and in Him Amen, **to the glory of God through us** (2 Corinthians 1:20).

All of God's promises are related to our futures. All of God's promises are pictures of His thoughts and intents for your life. They are pictures of God's goodness and your potential future. A promise builds expectation. Expectation is always about the future. But the last few words at the end of the verse give us an important key as to how this works: *"To the glory of God through us."*

> *Faith is the assurance that a seed will produce a harvest.*

We are the necessary visionaries who must determine to not only see the present but to see the future and *know where it comes from! Faith is the assurance that a seed will produce a harvest.* Faith understands that God's promises are the seeds He has given us for our futures. *Faith looks at a promise from God the same way a farmer looks at a seed.* The farmer sees a future harvest. Faith sees God's will fully accomplished. The future is in the seed, but it is dependent upon the heart and vision of you, the believer!

Think of it this way. Can a seed lie? While that may sound strange, give it some thought. Can a seed be anything other than what it was programmed to be from creation? Can it change its nature? In the right environment, can it fail to reproduce? We plant seeds because we know they cannot lie. We don't plant watermelon seeds with doubts about what will come up. We know that watermelons will be the result. Seeds don't lie. God's Word is the seed that carries the nature and purposes of God. His Word can't lie. Just as a farmer has full assurance that his corn seed will bring in a harvest of corn, the Christian can be equally assured that sowing God's promises into his life will bring forth the harvest that the promise has pictured.

Peter speaks to the purpose of God to deliver His people from the corruption in the world by means of promises.

> *Grace and peace be multiplied to you in the knowledge of God and of Jesus our Lord, as His divine power has given to us all things that pertain to life and godliness, through the knowledge of Him who called us by glory and virtue, by which have been given to us exceedingly great and precious promises,* **that through these** *you may be partakers of the divine nature, having escaped the corruption that is in the world through lust* (2 Peter 1:2-4).

Keeping in mind what we have discussed thus far, consider what God has given us to shape our futures. He has given us exceeding great and precious promises to help us escape a future of corruption and enjoy a future of abundant life (the divine nature). This is powerful!

His promises are the seeds of our futures. They are always yes and amen. They are programmed to reproduce (harvest) according to the nature of their Source. They are programmed for continual harvests of abundance. But only the visionary will see them and understand. The victim will consume what is on hand in the present and never understand how the future was wasted.

You will only sow toward what you can see. What you can't see will set the limitations of your life.

If you can't see fields of watermelons while you pick through the seeds of the one you are eating, you will never sow the seeds. Your life will be limited to getting watermelons from some other source because you had no vision for the seeds in your hand.

You will only sow in faith toward a harvest you believe in!

This is how we shape our futures. We must see with our spiritual eyes what God has already programmed into His creation and into His promises. You will only sow toward what you can see.

If you see tithing or giving as an obligation and a burden, you will never enter in with a cheerful heart. It will be money lost, not seed sown. A bad attitude can change the destiny for the life that was in the heart of God for you but was wasted for lack of vision. If you could actually see your resources as seeds and see the promises of God fulfilled in your life, you would give with joy and faith. You will give toward what you can see and what you believe in.

Many spend their money on the vain imaginations of the flesh. They are shaping their futures. Those with spiritual vision will sow their resources toward the promises of God, which are the divine seeds of abundant life. They have understood the promise that Jesus made:

> *Give, and it will be given to you: good measure, pressed down, shaken together, and running over will be put into your bosom. For with the same measure that you use, it will be measured back to you* (Luke 6:38).

This promise is valid in every area of life. It is a picture of God's original intention for increase in the earth. Lack in any area of life was never in God's purpose for His creation. Those who believe in God's goodness and abundance and who have understood the power of the seed will enter into God's way of doing things and shape their futures. *Your future is locked in the vision seeds in your heart right now.*

You will never sow in faith toward a harvest you don't believe in!

73

CHAPTER 5

WHAT CAN YOU SEE?

I HAVE increasingly realized how much of my future is dependent upon my spiritual sight. I can be carried through life on the river of culture, politics, and a fuzzy belief that God is somehow controlling all things, or I can choose to "see" the promises and purposes of God and become involved in the future that God has made possible.

What I see will determine what I focus on. If I choose to focus on perceived limitations, lack, insecurities, and wrongs suffered, I am shaping my future just as aggressively as if I were standing firm in my identity in Christ and laying hold of the promises of God. Our futures are being shaped by our attitudes, knowledge, and faith. We are continually sowing thought seeds, word seeds, and action seeds. We are sowing into one kingdom or another. *The nature of your harvest reveals where your seeds have been planted.*

> The nature of your harvest reveals where your seeds have been planted.

A powerful example of this can be found in the various stories of Jesus feeding the multitudes. The distinction between natural sight and spiritual sight is clearly revealed.

When it was evening, His disciples came to Him, saying, "This is a deserted place, and the hour is already late. Send the multitudes away, that they may go into the villages and buy themselves food." But Jesus said to them, "They do not need to go away. You give them something to eat." And they said to Him, "We have here only five loaves and two fish" (Matthew 14:15-17).

Keep in mind that everything involved in this story relates to the possible futures of thousands of people. These futures are immediate, not distant, but the principle involved is the same. Options for the future are presented and discussed. Only one future will be chosen.

Jesus asked the disciples to feed the multitude. To their minds this was obviously a ridiculous request. The amount of food needed or the money to buy so much food was not available. They were very committed to reporting to Jesus what the facts were, i.e., what they could "see." "We have here only five loaves and two fish." Even the words they chose to speak revealed their approach to the future: "We have *only.*"

They wanted to be sure that Jesus was completely aware of the lack.

This is a point to consider carefully when evaluating our own lives. We have all done this. When presented with an opportunity or challenge, our first response is typically a report on our natural inventory. We will speak of our lack of education or preparation, or our lack of resources or time, or we will make sure that everyone is aware of our limited comfort zone. Even when responding to the promises of God, "I have only" becomes our base of operations. Perhaps we will change the words to, "If you only knew my circumstances, my past, my needs, my challenges, etc." The name for this approach is "unbelief." Unbelief has destroyed more futures than we can know. The mentality of "I have only" has derailed the abundance of God in most of our lives.

Your future should be shaped by your vision and faith, not by your memories and fear. So often we allow our memories and human logic to have a suffocating influence over our vision for the future. It is a choice that many make without even realizing it. The disciples were guilty of this with the loaves and the fishes. Let's return to our story. Jesus is "seeing" the bread and fish from a different dimension.

> He said, "Bring them here to Me." Then He commanded the multitudes to sit down on the grass. And He took the five loaves and the two fish, and looking up to heaven, He blessed and broke and gave the loaves to the disciples; and the disciples gave to the multitudes. So they all ate and were filled, and they took up twelve baskets full of the

fragments that remained. Now those who had eaten were about five thousand men, besides women and children (Matthew 14:18-21).

We are speaking of vision, or spiritual sight. The disciples were convinced of lack. They were using their natural eyes and letting their senses determine the future. Jesus took the same resources and "looked up to heaven." *This is the key* to your future and the abundance of God! If Jesus had stopped to again count the loaves and fish and then declare to the disciples that they were right, there wasn't enough, the future lack of that day would have been confirmed. Do you realize that the future of one day can be the catalyst for a destiny? One day that is shaped by faith can be the beginning of the exceeding abundance of God for the rest of your life!

Your future should be shaped by your vision and faith, not by your memories and fear.

Jesus looked to heaven to "see" what God sees. He was already in faith when He commanded the multitudes to sit down. He was already committed. But He still took the time to "see" the possibilities from God's perspective.

Jesus then blessed the loaves and the fish. I want to include the story of a similar event found in Mark 8. While reading this a number of years ago, the Lord quickened me to see the keys of an abundant future. Read carefully.

*In those days, the multitude being very great and having nothing to eat, Jesus called His disciples to Him and said to them, "I have compassion on the multitude, because they have now continued with Me three days and have nothing to eat. And if I send them away hungry to their own houses, they will faint on the way; for some of them have come from afar." Then His disciples answered Him, "How can one satisfy these people with bread here in the wilderness?" He asked them, "How many loaves do you have?" And they said, "Seven." So He commanded the multitude to sit down on the ground. And He took the seven loaves and **gave thanks,** broke them and **gave them to His disciples to set before them**; and they set them before the multitude. They also had a few small fish; and **having blessed them,** He said to set them also before them. So they ate and were filled, and they took up seven large baskets of leftover fragments. Now those who had eaten were about four thousand. And He sent them away* (Mark 8:1-9).

I won't take the time to review the circumstances, because they are similar to our passage in Matthew 14. What caught my eye were the three keys revealed in this miracle of provision.

First, Jesus gave thanks for what He had. *"And He took the seven loaves and **gave thanks**."* Thankfulness for what we have will always open the door for the grace of God in our lives. Thankfulness is an attitude. It is a decision. Really, thankfulness is faith in action. It is the *"evidence of things not* *seen"* (Heb. 11:1). Jesus didn't complain about having limited resources. He gave thanks for what He had. He understood that what He had could be seen as not enough, or it could be seen as *seed!* The future is in the seeds of the present, but you must see it and be thankful.

Next, *Jesus used what He had.* "*He took the seven loaves and gave thanks, broke them and gave them to His disciples to set before them; and they set them before the multitude.*" Please notice that Jesus didn't wait to see multiplication before He passed out the bread. So often we declare that if we only had more, we would do more or give more. That way of thinking is natural and limited. It simply means that we haven't taken the time to look up to the Father and see what He sees. Jesus began passing out what was available before it looked like enough to the natural eye. He had already seen in the Spirit the multiplication of the bread.

I want you to understand something. The loaves and fish were not "magic" loaves and fish. They were not different from any other loaves and fish. The bread was baked by a baker and the fish were caught by a fisherman. The miracle wasn't about a special anointing on the loaves and fish. The miracle was a product of vision! Jesus chose to see with the Father's eyes, not with natural eyes. Spiritual vision changed the future. The multiplication was a result of seeing the abundance in the Spirit before it was seen in the natural. The future of thousands of people was established by the spiritual vision of abundance rather than the natural vision of lack. If you can get this, it will change your life!

But there is one more key in the story in Mark chapter 8. "*They also had a few small fish; **and having blessed them**, He* *said to set them also before them.*" First, we saw that Jesus gave thanks for what He had. He then used what He had before it appeared to be enough. He then blessed what He had.

What does this mean? What does it mean to bless something? Did you know there is power in your words? That death and life are in your words?

> *A man's stomach shall be satisfied from the fruit of his mouth, from the produce of his lips he shall be filled. Death and life are in the power of the tongue, and those who love it will eat its fruit* (Proverbs 18:20-21).

When Jesus blessed the seeming lack, He was releasing the same power and authority that God released when He created the earth. His blessing gave life to the loaves and fish. Paul reveals that God, Himself, speaks what He sees within Himself.

> *God, who gives life to the dead and **calls those things which do not exist as though they did*** (Romans 4:17).

To speak a blessing based on the spiritual vision of God's purpose and abundance is to release the very life and power of God into the situation. That is where the multiplication of the loaves and fish took place. *When something has life, it is designed to multiply.* The words of life, of thankfulness, and blessing released the supernatural power of God to multiply the existing lack and make it more than enough. This revelation is revolutionizing my life and it will revolutionize yours as well.

Take this into the world of money. I understand that many are quickly offended when the subject of money is brought into a discussion of anything Christian, but I'll take the risk. Does your money have the life of God in it, or is it dead and limited? Have you given thanks, blessed it, and put it to work, or are you hoarding it in fear? Both attitudes are shaping your future. We will visit this subject more, later in the book.

Your future has everything to do with your spiritual vision. Those who only see the watermelon with natural eyes will be limited to one watermelon. Those who see the abundance that God has designed into the watermelon seed will see the potential to have unlimited watermelons for years to come. Vision changes things. Words that spring from spiritual vision bring God's life into seemingly dead situations.

These truths can be carried over into every sphere of our lives. The seeds of prosperity for every area of your life already exist. *But do you see what you have as lack or do you see it as seeds of abundance?* Your vision determines the future. The seeds of health and healing are available to you right now, but do you see the seeds? Are you seeing and hearing the doctor's report, or are you looking up to heaven and seeing what God promises concerning your health? Where do you want your future to come from?

You will only sow in faith toward what you have seen from the Father.

Once you understand the incredible influence you can have over the future, you will be far more interested in seeing as God sees. What do you see for your marriage? If you aren't sowing seeds of love, giving, and forgiving in your marriage, it is because you haven't "seen" a better marriage in the Spirit. What are you sowing into your children? Are you sowing anger, strife, arguing, and neglect or words of life, encouragement, and blessing? Do you see your children succeeding and fulfilling their purpose in life? If you can see it, you will actively participate in it. If you are simply "along for the ride," you won't sow into your children to shape their futures. What are you sowing into your job or ministry? Are you sowing complaints, dread, and impatience or vision, faithfulness, and a positive attitude?

Your future hangs in the balance. You are far more involved in your future than you may have ever realized. *The seeds of the future are sown daily, and they reflect the eyes you are using to evaluate your life.* Spiritual eyes will see blessings and increase. Natural eyes will see limited resources and road-blocks. What you see is often what you will get.

When we can see the future with our spiritual eyes, our faith is activated and will carry us through to victory.

Whenever I have been challenged physically or am facing some other obstacle in my life, I have learned to switch over to my spiritual eyes. I look into the future, and if I can see myself healed, whole, prosperous, playing with my grand-kids, enjoying life with my wife, I know that I am going to pass through the storm successfully. Rather than focusing on the temporal challenge and becoming fearful and full of doubt, I endure by seeing the unseen.

As long as I can look into the future and see myself fulfill-ing my purpose in God, I know that any current challenge is temporal. It will pass. I will overcome. I can shape my future by choosing to see it through the potential of the seeds of His promises rather than the seeds of fear.

CHAPTER 6

SHAPED BY FEAR?

I WAS in the Boy Scouts and remember vividly being called upon at the last minute to speak at an awards ceremony. The other boy who was scheduled could not make it and the leader had chosen me. I was 12 years old and I was petrified. I had never spoken in front of people before, and I wasn't going to start now! As soon as we got to the Scout building, I separated from my parents, ran to a section of the building where the tents and supplies were stored, and hid under some folded tents. My dad couldn't find me until the ceremony was well underway and my scheduled part had passed.

That initial fear was only compounded the following year when I was chosen to moderate a school play (why me?), and I missed my cue, walked onto the stage too early, and the entire junior high roared with laughter as the teacher sent me off stage. As far as I was concerned, that was the end of public speaking for me! Of course, today sharing the gospel with hundreds and even thousands is the joy of my life.

How much of our life has been shaped by fear? The fear of death, disease, tragedy, rejection, and failure are powerful forces that can dominate our thoughts and steal our dreams. Fears such as public speaking, driving, high places, flying, sleeping in the dark, or not having enough money can continually shape our lives. Many of us probably don't realize how much we have allowed fear to frame us and limit us. Fear shapes the future just as powerfully as faith. The author of Hebrews mentions the bondage that can last for a lifetime due to fear.

> *And release those who through fear of death were all their lifetime subject to bondage* (Hebrews 2:15).

Fear was the initial reaction of Adam and Eve to the guilt they felt after sinning. Fear is the dominant force of the fallen human spirit. Fear is the product the world sells most effectively. The news succeeds by exploiting fear. The entertainment industry magnifies human fear in many of its movies and shows. Many of our decisions in life most likely take into consideration fears that have been sown into us, even if we are Christians. The torment of fear is a terrible dictator. John reveals the answer to the bondage of fear.

> *There is no fear in love; but perfect love casts out fear, because fear involves torment. But he who fears has not been made perfect in love* (1 John 4:18).

There is no fear in love! I doubt many of us have truly understood this. It is knowing God's love that sets us free from fear. Any fear in our lives is a signal that reveals a lack of the knowledge of God's love in that area. We can be free if we allow His love to fill us.

When we take the time to contemplate the power of fear, we can begin to understand why we often miss out on God's best for our lives. Is it possible to live free from fear? Can we really experience abundant life, joy, and peace in a fallen world? I believe that answer is "yes." His love has been shed abroad in our hearts and the potential to live free from fear is within. Paul reminded Timothy:

> *For God has not given us a spirit of fear, but of power and of love and of a sound mind* (2 Timothy 1:7).

In the same way that positive thoughts, words, and actions can shape our future according to the will of God, fearful thoughts, words, and actions can shape our futures according to the spirit of darkness. What many call wisdom is often fear wearing lipstick. If our so-called wisdom is not using the eyes of faith to see the unseen, it is probably just worldly wisdom establishing limitations based on fear.

Fear is never thankful.

Fear forms around what we see with our natural eyes, what we think about, how we speak, and how we act. It functions like faith but is going in the opposite direction. Fear doesn't look to God but looks to circumstances, feelings, and memories. *Fear is never thankful.*

Another way to understand fear is consider the subject of inferiority. If we feel inferior in any way to people, inferior to sickness, inferior to success or money, inferior because of our lack of education, inferior because of a divorce, inferior because of our race or place in society—those feelings of inferiority are simply the *symptoms* of fear. Inferiority on any level is a lack of revelation of our identity in Christ and our new nature—power, love, and a sound mind (see 2 Tim. 1:7).

Fear will always drain faith from your heart. It will never inspire you to believe God for more. *Fear will always rely on memories and not promises to guide you.* Fear will never move you toward increase, multiplication, and abundance. Fear cannot shape a future full of God's blessings. Jesus addressed this in the Sermon on the Mount.

> *Therefore* **do not worry about tomorrow**, *for tomorrow will worry about its own things. Sufficient for the day is its own trouble* (Matthew 6:34).

> *Fear will always rely on memories and not promises to guide you.*

Here we find worry linked to "tomorrow." Jesus's words are not a suggestion. The future should not be held hostage to the worries of today. The moment that worry and fear are given place, the seeds of limitation and loss are sown. The future becomes limited.

The psalmist understood the power of the revelation of God's heart for His people and how it could defeat fear.

The Lord is on my side; I will not fear. What can man do to me? (Psalm 118:6)

The decision to not fear is the fruit of a revelation of God's heart for you. *"The Lord is on my side."* Do you really believe that? Your future depends on it. Not only is He on your side, He lives in you! What can man do to you? Well, if you fear men, they can shape your future while you put God on a shelf. Solomon spoke of the power of the wisdom that comes from God in a similar declaration.

But whoever listens to me [wisdom] *will dwell safely, and will be secure,* **without fear of evil** (Proverbs 1:33).

Getting a true revelation of God's love is the only thing that can loosen the grip of fear in our lives. It is worth meditating on His love day and night until our minds and hearts are renewed and transformed to our true identity in Christ. His love will set you free. The more you know His love, the more you will identify all of the fears that have bound you and you will be able to be free once and for all. Knowing God's love is the antidote to fear. David said it this way:

I sought the Lord, and He heard me, and delivered me from all my fears (Psalm 34:4).

As mentioned already, most of us have dealt with the enemy of fear in the area of inferiority. Many feel inferior to other people, inferior to sickness, inferior to money, inferior in our educational status, our marital status, or our means of making a living. Quiet personalities can feel inferior to the more outgoing. In the church, women are often made to feel inferior to men (due to a wrong understanding of Scripture). All of these are symptoms of fear.

Inferiority is a fruit of the root of fear. You may not think you live in fear, but to the degree you feel inferior to others or to circumstances, you *are* living in fear.

> *For God has not given us a spirit of fear, but of power and of love and of a sound mind* (2 Timothy 1:7).

Our new creation reality is that the spirit of fear (and, by extension, inferiority) is no longer a part of our recreated nature. Our new creation nature is one of power, love, and a sound mind. But if we don't embrace that truth and we allow our past to dominate our present, we can continue to live our lives full of fear and inferiority.

When the doctor says you have a terminal disease, do you feel inferior to the disease? That is fear and it will shape your future. When your bank account declares that you don't have enough, do you feel inferior to the power of money? That is also fear and will shape your future.

Something that set me free a long time ago was the realization that I was just as valuable to God as anyone else on this planet. My faith has just as much potential as anyone else's faith. My status in the Kingdom comes from Jesus in me, not from my education, money, or personality.

I have shared of my fear of public speaking. Today, I understand who Christ is in me. Today, my favorite thing to do is share the Word with people. I can't imagine what my future would have been had I succumbed to the fear of public speaking. The future that God had for me had to be released from the bondage of fear by understanding His love for me. Love motivates me to speak publicly. Fear lost, love won!

A future of abundant life, love, joy, and peace has everything to do with truly knowing how much God loves you. His love will bring the confident assurance of a future that is blessed in spite of the challenges that may exist. We will be far more prepared to shape the future from a place of peace and rest in His love than we will from a place of fear, anxiety, and inferiority.

As we continue in our quest to shape the future according to God's love and purposes, we must be sure that we have a true image of God. In the next chapter we will consider some wrong understandings of God that paralyze the future of many.

CHAPTER 7

THE GOSPEL OF CLICHÉS

WHEN we speak of the future we are immediately faced with our concepts of God, our understanding of man, and our perception of the enemy. Our beliefs about God, ourselves, and the devil will activate our faith or suffocate our potential. Sadly, religion has created a culture of wrong thinking in these areas, and the result is often fatalism. Fatalism is a paralyzing force that limits man's role in life to that of a spectator with almost no part to play. Futures have been lost through a fatalistic approach to life. As has been mentioned earlier, such a theological position has been marketed as "faith," but is really anything but faith. It is resignation disguised by common clichés. Let's look at some of the clichés that can steal the future.

CLICHÉ #1: "GOD IS IN CONTROL."

This is a typical response by many Christians to any event in the world that seems tragic or incomprehensible. It is meant to convey that while world events, tragedies, sicknesses, and death may be mysterious to us, we can take comfort because God has everything under control.

I know that some readers will react to this chapter because the idea of God not having control of all things is shocking and even considered to be heresy by some. Please bear with me for a moment as we try and understand how damaging this concept is.

I would suggest that God has everything under control in heaven, and the new heaven and the new earth, because everyone and everything will be fully and willingly submitted to Him. On this earth, however, we see corruption, death, tragedy, and darkness. Is God controlling these things? What does that mean? Is God orchestrating human suffering and tragedy?

Why do we glibly declare that God is in control, but He doesn't even control those of us who claim to be filled with His Spirit? Does God force you to obey the law, pay your taxes, drive the speed limit, and deny the flesh? Aren't those your personal decisions? Is God controlling you? And yet, we are to believe that God has everything else and everyone else under control? If God isn't controlling you, then what exactly is He controlling? Is He sending hurricanes, earthquakes, wildfires, and other destructive events into the world for some divine purpose? Does God raise up terrorists to spread death and fear? Is God controlling terrorists? When we say that "God is in control," what are we implying?

As has been mentioned earlier, God gave the earth to man (see Gen. 1:26-28; Ps. 115:16; 8:4-6). This truth is the foundation for understanding the nature of God, the nature of man, and the purpose of redemption. Man was created in God's image and created to have dominion over God's creation. Sin separated man from God's life and purpose and left the earth under the dominion of Satan. John recognized this even after the victory of the cross. There is still an enemy in the world.

> *We know that we are of God, and **the whole world lies under the sway of the wicked one*** (1 John 5:19).

If the whole world lies under the sway of the wicked one, are we to believe that God is controlling the wicked one? If so, why did Jesus come to defeat him and his works?

> *For this purpose the Son of God was manifested, that He might **destroy the works of the devil*** (1 John 3:8).

To suggest that God controls all things places full responsibility for sickness, death, tragedies, wars, natural disasters, child abuse, and every other evil in His lap. It makes God the perpetrator or a willing accomplice of human suffering. It leaves our future in a murky, mystical realm of uncertainty in which we become simple pawns. If God is in control and the world is out of control, why should I expect anything positive in this life? For this reason, many reject the gospel, and many believers learn to accept the works of the enemy and the darkness of fallen humanity as the sovereign will of God. And then they declare that God is love!

As a result, many live their lives expecting loss, failure, sickness, tragedy, and perhaps an untimely death. They are allowing the fallen world to shape their futures.

The truth is far different. Once we recognize that Adam's sin is the beginning of all evil in the earth, we can begin to shape our futures according to Jesus's words and redemptive work. Jesus's redemptive work on the cross restored man to a place of potential dominion and, in fact, finds us seated with Him far above all principality and power!

> *Which He worked in Christ when He raised Him from the dead and seated Him at His right hand in the heavenly places, far above all principality and power and might and dominion, and every name that is named, not only in this age but also in that which is to come. **And He put all things under His feet, and gave Him to be head over all things to the church*** (Ephesians 1:20-22).

> *And raised us up together, and made us sit together in the heavenly places in Christ Jesus* (Ephesians 2:6).

But aren't we destined to suffer in this world? Don't Jesus and Paul both speak of suffering? Yes, but the suffering does not come from God. After the cross, suffering is always referred to in the context of persecution for the sake of the gospel. Suffering is never taught as the work of God for the benefit of the believer. Once we understand that the suffering promised the Christian concerns only persecution for our faith, the picture becomes clearer. Remember an earlier verse that we have discussed.

*By which have been given to us exceedingly great and precious promises, that through these you may be partakers of the divine nature, **having escaped the corruption that is in the world through lust*** (2 Peter 1:4).

The corruption that is in the world through lust is a different kind of suffering from the persecution for our faith. Escaping corruption is God's heart for His children. *His promises are given precisely to equip the believer to shape a future that is not a part of the corruption of the world.*

There is a difference between suffering for our faith and suffering the corruption that is in the world through lust. Jesus spoke of the persecution that would accompany the last days before His return.

Then they will deliver you up to tribulation and kill you, and you will be hated by all nations for My name's sake (Matthew 24:9).

If you are suffering and it isn't persecution for your faith, then it shouldn't be embraced as God's will. When this difference isn't understood, it is possible to suffer from living in a fallen, corrupt world and think that you are suffering for His Name's sake. But this is simply not true. The promises of God were given so that we escape the corruption that the world suffers. Except for persecution for our faith, we should be living victorious lives and actively shaping our futures.

Even Christians who are suffering in oppressive countries and political systems can still prosper spiritually, mentally, emotionally, and relationally. They can still shape their futures. Paul shaped his future even while in prison!

When we get the revelation that God gave dominion to man, we can begin to cooperate with His purposes in the earth. We are called to reign in life! Paul declared clearly what grace and the gift of righteousness are meant to accomplish in the life of a believer.

> ...*Much more those who receive abundance of grace and of the gift of righteousness **will reign in life** through the One, Jesus Christ* (Romans 5:17).

Reigning in life hardly resembles the passive resignation that so many Christians have accepted. We are called to still the storms, heal the sick, cast out demons, and extend the Kingdom. This is why Jesus said:

> *Most assuredly, I say to you, he who believes in Me, the works that I do he will do also; and greater works than these he will do, because I go to My Father* (John 14:12).

Wouldn't greater works change the destinies of those lives touched by such works? Wouldn't those believers doing such works be living out a different future than one of passive resignation? It all goes back to the story of the watermelon seeds. We can spit them or plant them. We can reign in life or let life reign over us. We have the "seeds" of reigning within, but will we use them?

We aren't called to sit back and respond with clichés to the suffering around us or in our own lives. It is time to submit to the true knowledge of God; resist Satan, sin, and corruption; and reign in life! James tells us:

> *Therefore submit to God. Resist the devil and he will flee from you* (James 4:7).

If causing the devil to flee doesn't impact the future, then what does?

One verse destroys the argument that God is controlling all things:

> *For this purpose the Son of God was manifested, that He might destroy the works of the devil* (1 John 3:8).

In one brief sentence we discover that there is a devil, he has works, his works are worthy of destruction, and Jesus came to destroy the devil's works! If God is controlling all things, He is working against Himself!

No! There is a devil whose works (lies, oppression, sickness, destruction, poverty, etc.) are not of God, and Jesus came to destroy those works. Everything that happens in this world is not God's will.

CLICHÉ #2: "EVERYTHING HAPPENS FOR A REASON."

A typical response to bad things happening is that they "happen for a reason." We see this phrase used over and over on TV, in interviews, and even in our churches. Once again, the believer assumes there is a divine purpose in everything that happens. The fact that there is an enemy whose purpose is to steal, kill, and destroy; and that we have been given the armor of God to withstand evil; and the fact that we can resist the devil and he will flee; and the fact that we have been commissioned to do greater works than Jesus; and the fact that we have been given His promises in order to escape the corruption of the world are either overlooked or ignored. It is much easier to sit back and declare that there is a divine reason behind all tragedy, loss, failure, sickness, premature death, and heartache. There is a default belief system in many that rests in the idea of a cosmic, divine influence over the earth that mysteriously is bringing about God's divine will through the catastrophes that happen in the world.

But what about Romans 8:28? Let's take a look at that verse.

And we know that all things work together for good to those who love God, to those who are the called according to His purpose (Romans 8:28).

While some use this verse to assume that all bad things are from God, what is being said falls in line with the subject of this book. When we love God according to His true nature and we walk in His purpose to reign in life and extend the Kingdom, *God will honor our vision and faith and bring good from negative circumstances.*

So much of this tremendous promise depends on how we see God, how we see ourselves, and how we see our role in His Kingdom. The same promises that He has given so that we escape the corruption in the world are the ones that will cause things to work together for good (see 2 Pet. 1:2-4). But a passive Christian who accepts bad things as having a divine purpose will live a fatalistic life that is similar to many of the world's empty religions. There isn't much difference between "if Allah wills it," and "if it be Thy will," when said in resignation. Fate is not faith. "If it be Thy will" should be a statement of submission to God's purpose, not a statement of resignation to the forces of darkness.

The Bible declares that things happen according to the spiritual law of sowing and reaping. As we have discussed earlier, God created all living things with the "seed principle" for multiplication. If we sow to the flesh, we will reap corruption. If we sow to the Spirit, we will reap life. That concept is all about the future!

> For he who sows to his flesh will of the flesh reap corruption, but he who sows to the Spirit will of the Spirit reap everlasting life (Galatians 6:8).

"If it be Thy will" should be a statement of submission to God's purpose, not a statement of resignation to the forces of darkness.

Once we grasp this spiritual law, it is easy to look at the world and realize the loss, suffering, sickness, and tragedy that many are experiencing have nothing to do with God's will, but everything to do with reaping the corruption of sowing to the flesh. Living a life focused on the lust of the flesh, self-centeredness, strife, unforgiveness, anxiety, fear, ego, greed, etc. is shaping the future. Seedtime and harvest are at work. To say that everything has a purpose is to willfully choose ignorance and to throw away God's empowering plan for abundant life.

The works of the flesh described in Galatians 5 are the reasons that many bad things happen:

> *Now the works of the flesh are evident, which are: adultery, fornication, uncleanness, lewdness, idolatry, sorcery, hatred, contentions, jealousies, outbursts of wrath, selfish ambitions, dissensions, heresies, envy, murders, drunkenness, revelries, and the like; of which I tell you beforehand, just as I also told you in time past, that those who practice such things will not inherit the kingdom of God* (Galatians 5:19-21).

Adultery, fornication murders, drunkenness, hatred, etc. are inherently evil and almost always are the beginning of heartache, suffering, sickness, and loss. One of the reasons so many bad things happen in the earth is due to the lust of the flesh. God is not controlling your flesh. That is your job and He has given you His Spirit to do it!

> *For if you live according to the flesh you will die; but if by the Spirit you put to death the deeds of the body, you will live* (Romans 8:13).

Two futures are possible in the verse above—life and death. *The Spirit has been given to believers to shape the future toward life.*

Another reason that bad things happen is that God's people are destroyed for lack of knowledge.

> *My people are destroyed for lack of knowledge* (Hosea 4:6).

Ignorance of God's ways is a major reason why bad things happen. If we believe we have no part to play in shaping our lives and our futures, we have basically given in to fatalism. We must then choose to believe that the work of the enemy (steal, kill, and destroy) is actually the work of God.

The outcome is to always consciously or subconsciously blame God for everything while ignoring our own role in the chain of events that brought forth disaster.

CLICHÉ #3: "GOD ALLOWS EVIL."

One of the most horrible answers to evil and suffering in the world is that "God allows it." Inherent in this approach, God becomes the perpetrator or an accessory to crimes against humanity. Such a belief system effectively challenges the justice system of any civilized society. If God allows evil, what right do we have to punish evildoers? Paul's explanation of God's purpose for civil government in Romans 13 puts civil government at odds with God Himself, if He allows evil.

> *For rulers are not a terror to good works, but to evil. Do you want to be unafraid of the authority? Do what is good, and you will have praise from the same. **For he is God's minister** to you for good. But if you do evil, be afraid; for he does not bear*

the sword in vain; **for he is God's minister, an avenger to execute wrath on him who practices evil** (Romans 13:3-4).

It is God who ordained civil government as an avenger to execute wrath upon those who do evil. How is it that some teach that God Himself is allowing or causing evil? He would be violating His own nature and decree for civil government. If God is a perpetrator or accessory to evil, then under His own decree He would be a candidate for punishment!

If evil is from God for His own divine purposes, it should be celebrated, not criminalized. For some reason, nonsense makes sense to religious minds.

The truth is that God did *not* allow sin and evil into the earth. Man allowed it. God created man in His own image and gave man the power to make choices. Everything God created was good. There was no sin, no death, no sickness, no war, no natural disasters, and no suffering in God's creation. God specifically told Adam and Eve to *not* eat of the Tree of the Knowledge of Good and Evil. *He did not allow evil, but He did allow them to choose.*

We must understand that the nature of God is good. Good has one Source—God. Evil is the absence of good just as darkness is the absence of light. *Evil is the consequence of independence from God.* It was never God's will that His creation live independently from Him. Even Jesus in His mission as the Son of Man was fully dependent on the Father. Jesus declared that He could do nothing except what He received from His Father.

> *Then Jesus answered and said to them, "Most*
> *assuredly, I say to you, **the Son can do nothing of***
> ***Himself,** but what He sees the Father do; for what-*
> *ever He does, the Son also does in like manner"*
> (John 5:19).

Jesus was entirely dependent on the Father for everything He said and He did. This was also God's will in the beginning with Adam and Eve. God did not cause or choose their independence, nor the tragic consequences. Adam and Eve were created to live in dependence on God but chose independence. It is interesting that in Jesus's life of dependence on God, He never allowed evil, never caused evil, and spent His earthly ministry undoing evil and teaching men to live in harmony with the Father. Jesus didn't "allow" evil. He overcame it!

> *How God anointed Jesus of Nazareth with the Holy*
> *Spirit and with power, who went about **doing good***
> ***and healing all who were oppressed by the devil,***
> *for God was with Him* (Acts 10:38).

Note that God's presence with Jesus brought an end to evil and established that which is good. The cliché that "God allowed it" is a direct contradiction to that which is revealed in the ministry of Jesus.

Sin entered the world through man, not through God. Paul referred to this.

> *Therefore, just **as through one man sin entered***
> ***the world,** and death through sin* (Romans 5:12).

What God allows is for man to choose dependence upon Him and live. If man chooses darkness and death, God will respect that decision, but He is not responsible for the heartache and suffering that will come from such decisions.

God does not allow evil. *He allows man to choose dependence or independence, and He will respect those decisions.* Evil is man's fault, not God's. Your future is in your hands. Blaming God for evil is to give up your right to shape your future.

CLICHÉ #4: "THE LORD GIVES, AND THE LORD TAKES AWAY."

The Lord gave, and the Lord has taken away; blessed be the name of the Lord (Job 1:21).

Most Christians should know that God did not make this statement. This was Job's understanding of Satan's attack against him. But what about the declaration that follows?

In all this Job did not sin nor charge God with wrong (Job 1:22).

It could be said that Job had not charged God *yet,* but he was about to accuse God dozens of times in the following chapters. His integrity transformed into bitterness. At the end of the book of Job, Job repented for his ignorance, and this statement was certainly in need of repentance.

Therefore I have uttered what I did not understand (Job 42:3).

> *I have heard of You by the hearing of the ear, but now my eye sees You.* ***Therefore I abhor myself, and repent in dust and ashes*** (Job 42:5-6).

There was integrity in his heart, but a serious lack of knowledge in his first declaration (see Job 1:21). Nevertheless, many of God's children quote "the Lord gives and the Lord takes away" more frequently than any other verse in the Bible. The book of Job has become more important than the four gospels for many. Identifying with Job's sufferings seems to bring comfort for some reason.

The truth of the matter is that God gives, and the devil takes away. Jesus declared that the thief comes to steal, kill, and destroy. Jesus came so that we might have abundant life!

> *The thief does not come except to steal, and to kill, and to destroy. I have come that they may have life, and that they may have it more abundantly* (John 10:10).

Once again, those who witness or experience loss and tragedy usually want to feel justified and affirmed in their experience. What better way than to blame God? Most may not realize they are blaming God, but when they justify their losses as a divine "whim," they are effectively putting the blame on God.

In order to move from darkness to light, we must have a revelation of the new creation and the better covenant established on better promises. The writer of Hebrews declared, concerning Jesus:

But now He has obtained a more excellent minis-
*try, inasmuch as He is also Mediator of **a better***
covenant, which was established on better prom-
ises (Hebrews 8:6).

Our covenant is not based upon our behavior, but rather on Jesus's redemptive work on the cross. God gave Jesus to the world in order that sin and death might not steal, kill, and ultimately destroy us. Until we understand redemption, we will struggle with the idea of shaping our futures.

God has always been the giver. Let's consider some verses that reveal God's will, His nature, and His heart for His children.

He cannot be tempted with evil, nor does He tempt any with evil. James reminded us:

Let no one say when he is tempted, "I am tempted
by God"; for God cannot be tempted by evil, nor
does He Himself tempt anyone (James 1:13).

Every good gift comes from God:

Every good gift and every perfect gift is from above,
and comes down from the Father of lights, with
whom there is no variation or shadow of turning
(James 1:17).

And all of His promises are yes and amen:

For all the promises of God in Him are Yes, and
in Him Amen, to the glory of God through us (2
Corinthians 1:20).

It is His divine promises that allow us to escape the corruption of the world.

> *Grace and peace be multiplied to you in the knowledge of God and of Jesus our Lord, as His divine power has given to us all things that pertain to life and godliness, through the knowledge of Him who called us by glory and virtue, by which have been given to us exceedingly great and precious promises, that through these you may be partakers of the divine nature, having escaped the corruption that is in the world through lust* (2 Peter 1:2-4).

He gave us His Son and has determined to freely give us all things.

> *He who did not spare His own Son, but delivered Him up for us all, how shall He not with Him also freely give us all things?* (Romans 8:32)

The Spirit of God abides in us that we might know the things that He has freely given us.

> *Now we have received, not the spirit of the world, but the Spirit who is from God, that we might know the things that have been freely given to us by God* (1 Corinthians 2:12).

If you are walking and living in the Spirit, you should be growing in the knowledge of every good thing that has been given to us. Only carnal Christians will look at God as the "taker," not the giver. Let's look at one more example.

Jesus declared if we seek first His Kingdom and righteousness, everything we need in this life will be added to us.

> But seek first the kingdom of God and His righteousness, and all these things shall be added to you (Matthew 6:33).

The list could go on and on. The point is, God is *not the thief!* Yet in spite of the overwhelming evidence of God's heart and God's goodness, when something bad happens many Christians will immediately quote, "The Lord gives, and the Lord takes away." It is virtual schizophrenia! God is for us and His promises are alive and active. One of the major things standing between us and abundant life is our gospel of clichés that promotes fatalism and passivity. Rather than learning to reign in life, many are content to say, "Whatever will be, will be." This can promote passivity rather than overcoming faith. The future that was possible becomes impossible when you believe that God is working with the devil or orchestrating the tragedies of life for some mysterious purpose.

CLICHÉ #5: "GOD MOVES IN MYSTERIOUS WAYS."

The mother of all religious clichés might be this one. The idea is that God is mysterious, and we are simple pawns in His celestial game. What right do we have to understand anything? "He has it all under control. Everything happens for a reason. He allows evil. He gives and takes away", and just to make sure that we wash our hands of all responsibility we declare, "He moves in mysterious ways."

Nevertheless, Jesus made it clear that if you have seen Him, you have seen the Father:

> *Jesus said to him, "Have I been with you so long, and yet you have not known Me, Philip? He who has seen Me has seen the Father; so how can you say, 'Show us the Father'?" (John 14:9)*

Jesus is God in the flesh. His words and actions perfectly reveal the Father. There is no more mystery! If you want to know what God is like, look at Jesus. He went about doing good and healing all *because God was with Him* (see Acts 10:38). Where God is, goodness and healing exist.

Actually, the mystery resides in the hearts of those who have chosen ignorance and fatalism. They have refused to be transformed by the renewing of their minds (see Rom. 12:2). They have not sought out wisdom and spiritual understanding (see Eph. 1:17-18). The thought of accepting the responsibility for reigning in life overwhelms them. Living by clichés is much easier.

Your expectations in life will follow your core beliefs. If you believe that God is schizophrenic and mysterious, you should expect a life of questions and loss. Clichés will be your only solution. When you understand that God has given you His Name, His blood, His Spirit, His Word, His better Covenant, His promises, His armor, His faith, and the keys to His Kingdom, *you will begin to cooperate with Him and enforce His will in your life.* You can shape your future! You don't have to be a perpetual victim.

It is time to expect God's blessings in your life. It is time to expect to do God's works. It is time to resist the enemy. It is time to walk in your divine authority over the enemy, sickness, and loss. Drop the clichés and get to know God. He has given you dominion. Don't give it back to the devil!

CHAPTER 8

THE SEEDS OF LIFE

W HAT do you have now that can become the seeds of your future? Many times we evaluate our current circumstances in terms of what we don't have, and perhaps we are a little jealous of those who seem to have more. What we are looking at are temporal, physical things, but we are missing the eternal, invisible things that hold the future in seed form.

So much of the future is simply a harvest of our thoughts, words, actions, attitudes, and choices. We are actively sowing toward the future every day whether we think about it or not. We may also be allowing others to sow into us their perceptions, attitudes, and words as well. We must consider the seeds of the media including the news and Hollywood. Which seeds of corruption and degradation have you accepted into your thinking?

Politics is a very sensitive issue for many, which carries seeds of frustration, bitterness, and anger. Political debate can be a harvest of emotions and beliefs that carry the seeds of the future. Whether we care to admit it or not, the future is being shaped by those politicians who have a vision to shape it. The seeds of the world we will live in ten years from now are being sown today. Are you willing to live in a future being shaped by the powers of darkness, or would you like to be actively involved in shaping your own future?

The idea of proactively shaping our futures may be new to some, but it is happening whether we like it or not. Even passivity and resignation are a type of proactive involvement. *Non-involvement is a choice and every choice is a seed.*

Everything in life can be a seed. As discussed earlier, it is the visionary who determines if something is a seed or a temporary resource. Eating a watermelon can be a one-time event or it can be the beginning of a hobby or a business. The visionary decides. Your future is waiting for your vision!

> *Your future is waiting for your vision!*

Understanding this concept in every area of life is the difference between those who shape a future of blessing and those who simply allow life to happen and accept whatever comes their way.

How I sow into my marriage and into my family is shaping their futures and mine. Words and actions of love, giving, sacrifice, and time are all seeds that carry a message and a potential. So are words and actions of frustration, anger, and fear. We may not even be aware that we are sowing into someone until we hear them years later sharing how a certain action we did or word we said impacted them.

I have been approached many times by those who have heard me teach, and they have explained how my teaching from years ago has helped them, healed them, or set them free. I was sowing from the grace of God that He has given to me, but the news of the harvest reached me much later. Ministry is all about seedtime and harvest.

Children are a blank slate, created to have their trusting hearts filled with the love and encouragement of a parent. They are created to believe the words of their parents. Parents are shaping the futures of their children every day. Anger, strife, lies, and neglect are powerful seeds that will reproduce according to their kind (nature). Just as a diet of sugary products will have an impact on their ability to learn and function, a diet of abuse or neglect will do the same. *Wise parents must recognize that every day in the life of a child is a fresh field that waits to be sown with seeds of faith, hope and love.* The harvest of our seeds will become apparent in the teen years and early adulthood.

The government and local school boards are very proactive in sowing their agendas into our children. They are expecting a harvest that fits their worldview. What are we as parents doing to influence our kids? Who will be to blame for the children who grow up to be confused, angry, and conformed to this world?

As you can see, the futures of individuals, families, and even countries are not set in stone, certainly not by God. *The future is nothing more than a set of influences that bear the nature of their source (light or darkness) and have been allowed to reproduce over and over again.* You can allow yourself to be shaped and conformed, or you can choose to do the shaping and forming.

The most powerful influence that is available to shape the future is the Word of God. In the beginning was the Word, and God sent His Word (Jesus) full of grace and truth.

> *And the Word became flesh and dwelt among us, and we beheld His glory, the glory as of the only begotten of the Father, full of grace and truth* (John 1:14).

It is the grace of God that makes provision for every need of mankind, and it is His truth that will set us free from the bondage to corruption. Bondage to sin and corruption *is* a future, but not the future God has in mind for anyone. Grace has equipped the believer to walk in freedom, righteousness, authority, and faith. It is worth repeating that the equipping of God includes:

- The Name of Jesus

- The Holy Spirit

- The Blood of Jesus

- The Better Covenant

- The Word of God

- The Promises of God

- The Armor of God

- The Gifts of the Spirit

- The Keys of the Kingdom

- The New Creation

These are the seeds of life, the seeds of a possible future. How can anyone look at this list and believe that passivity and resignation represent the Gospel message? I can only imagine God's grief at seeing His children battered by the enemy in a fallen world while they believe their resignation and suffering are true faith.

As I mentioned earlier, seedtime and harvest, or sowing and reaping, is one of the clearest teachings in the Bible. Not only is it a natural law, it is a spiritual law. In fact, the natural law of sowing and reaping is a manifestation of the spiritual law that sustains it. What is seen was not made out of things that are visible (see Heb. 11:3).

Sowing means giving something you have in order to bless others. You can sow time, resources, attitude, love, service, or even a smile. We sow time and love to reap healthy family relationships. We sow wisdom to solve problems. We sow words to bring forgiveness, health, and vision. We sow resources to release abundance.

A harvest is every good thing that God brings into your life. A new opportunity, a new relationship, an idea, a vision, or a blessing of resources are all harvests. They represent blessings from seeds sown in the past and carry their own seeds for the future.

Giving is the very nature of God. God is Love and Love gives. God had a Son, but He wanted a family. He gave His Son in order to reap you and me.

Elijah demanded food and water of the widow woman. Her offering was the seed that opened the door to her survival for over three years (see 1 Kings 17:8-16).

Jesus received the offering of bread and fish and multiplied it to feed 5,000.

Jesus said to give and it would be given unto us pressed down, shaken together, and running over (see Luke 6:38).

God saw the giving and heard the prayers of Cornelius and sent an angel to change his destiny (see Acts 10:1-8).

Paul encouraged cheerful giving and explained how such giving would unleash "all grace" in order that the givers would have an abundance for every good deed (see 2 Cor. 9:6-11).

Your seed is a door to your destiny. Everything can be a seed. Your thoughts, words, actions, and resources can all be sown into the Kingdom or into the darkness of the world, and they will multiply according to their kind. *Your confession of Jesus Christ was a seed that forever changed your eternal future.* It can also change your future in this life if you choose to be a visionary with all that God has given you.

Grace flows from the principle of the seed, but *you will never sow toward a harvest you don't believe in.* Future provision and abundance are found in the seeds of our thoughts, words, actions, attitudes, and resources. Increase is designed into every seed, but if you don't see the harvest God has promised, you won't sow in faith. You'll simply live a life of resignation.

Let's consider the Parable of the Sower as we continue to discuss the seeds of life and their potential.

Therefore hear the parable of the sower: When anyone hears the word of the kingdom, and does not understand it, then the wicked one comes and snatches away what was sown in his heart. This is he who received seed by the wayside. But he who received the seed on stony places, this is he who hears the word and immediately receives it with joy; yet he has no root in himself, but endures only for a while. For when tribulation or persecution arises because of the word, immediately he stumbles. Now he who received seed among the thorns is he who hears the word, and the cares of this world and the deceitfulness of riches choke the word, and he becomes unfruitful. But he who received seed on the good ground is he who hears the word and understands it, who indeed bears fruit and produces: some a hundredfold, some sixty, some thirty (Matthew 13:18-23).

The seed in this parable is the Word of God (see Luke 8:11). A seed is programmed to accomplish a certain purpose. Every seed has its specific destiny locked within. But not just a one-time destiny lies within a seed. There are infinite destinies (harvests) that are possible. In the Parable of the Sower, we find the seed (in this case the gospel of the Kingdom) and different types of soil. As we read of the different results in the different kinds of soil, it is quickly apparent that the seed is dependent on the type of soil into which it is sown. Poor soil will bring forth poor results. It isn't the fault of the seed, but rather the condition of the soil that determines the future. The soil is the human heart. This is why the writer of Proverbs reminds us:

Keep your heart with all diligence, for out of it spring the issues of life (Proverbs 4:23).

The heart is the real factory of the future. The human heart generates our thoughts, our words, our actions, and our attitudes. The human heart either receives or rejects the Word of God. Our futures reside in our hearts in seed form. The question is, what is the seed that is growing there? Is it the Word of God and the promises of God, or is it the corruption of the world?

There may be the good seed of God's Word in our hearts, but if it is competing with the cares of this life, the good seed may be choked out. It isn't the fault of the seed. A heart filled with the seeds of the world—such as fear, anxiety, bitterness, strife, or unbelief—is going to sow those seeds into the future and lose the possibilities that God had purposed from before time began (see 2 Tim. 1:9).

Thankfully, it only takes a moment of revelation and understanding to allow our hearts to be touched by God and transformed into a harvest of God's abundance. Many past seeds that we have sown from fear and strife can be overwhelmed by the grace of God's love, forgiveness, and His promises. And His seeds are ready for planting!

A seed is a harvest in waiting. It is a future ready to be unlocked. It can be a container of love, joy, peace, health, and prosperity, or it can hold fear, envy, bitterness, limitations, sickness, and loss. God has given His seeds of abundant life to the sower—the believer.

*Now may **He who supplies seed to the sower,** and bread for food, supply and multiply the seed you* *have sown and increase the fruits of your righteousness* (2 Corinthians 9:10).

Every harvest contains provision for the present and seed for the future. Some only see the present and neglect the potential that is within the grace of the seed.

The enemy and the world have given seed as well. We will sow from one source or the other. God has given us His nature, His Word, His promises, His love, peace, and joy, and so much more! In each gift live the seeds of the future. Your life will harvest that which is in your heart and sown into your world. It is a spiritual law. You are shaping your future whether you know it or not.

Your tomorrows are in your seeds.

Your tomorrows are in your seeds.

CHAPTER 9

NEED OR VISION?

D O you believe that you have enough to live the abundant life? Some may ask, "Enough what?" "All I see is lack." "All I feel is my affliction."

When we understand how the Kingdom works, we will realize that more than enough for every need is available right now. The problem might be our focus.

If I could give one word of counsel that would fit every possible situation and challenge, it would be this: *Stop focusing on your need and start recognizing your seed!*

It isn't our need that deserves our focus, time, and attention. Most of us, when challenged by a negative circumstance, sickness, or need, focus on that need. We take every thought captive to the need. We meditate on it day and night. We talk about it to others. Our lives revolve around the problem and pain.

What is driving your life? What do you wake up thinking about every day?

Far too often we are being driven by the needs of the day. Our minds are consumed with planning how we can accomplish as many things as possible while knowing that it will never be enough. We may approach the day with anxiety, dread, or even fear. "If I can just get through today, perhaps I can breathe more easily tomorrow." And yet, tomorrow is usually just like today. Paul gave us a powerful clue as to how we should approach our lives.

> *For our light affliction, which is but for a moment, is working for us a far more exceeding and eternal weight of glory, **while we do not look at the things which are seen, but at the things which are not seen.** For the things which are seen are temporary, but the things which are not seen are eternal* (2 Corinthians 4:17-18).

Most of us have been taught to foresee needs, respond to needs, and do everything we can to meet every need. We live in a world of perpetual needs. Paul would call this "our light affliction, which is but for a moment." While the needs may be important, should they be our singular purpose on this earth? Is there anything bigger or higher that we should be living for?

Is it possible that in our busyness, we are missing God's vision for our lives? Rather than living our lives focused on needs, could we not rather look at the unseen and pursue the vision God has placed in our hearts? God had a vision for Paul and counted him faithful while Paul was persecuting the church! Paul's vision when Jesus called out to him was not God's vision, but God awakened His vision in Paul with a word. Paul was driven by the need to exterminate Christians, but God awakened the vision of taking the gospel around the world!

In the midst of our busy lives, it is still possible that a word from God can awaken us as well. Are we living to simply meet needs or are we living according to a vision? Both approaches carry a future within.

Needs are motivators that keep our natural eyes focused on the temporal. Human logic, reasoning, planning, and worry often keep us glued to the obvious needs we all have. Jesus spoke of this as well:

> *Therefore do not worry, saying, "What shall we eat?" or "What shall we drink?" or "What shall we wear?"* (Matthew 6:31)

Being driven by needs is common. It is also the reason so few ever step into their true purpose and destiny. How did Jesus finish this thought?

> *But **seek first the kingdom of God** and His righteousness, and all these things shall be added to you* (Matthew 6:33).

In other words, *be driven by your vision, not by your needs.* Seek first His Kingdom. Look at the eternal. It is in pursuing God's vision that our needs will be met.

Most inventions, scientific advancements, incredible buildings, and dramatic accomplishments were brought forth by those who didn't focus on their need, but rather on something within that motivated them. Most great inventions and technological advancements actually had others in mind, not self. In the process of the visionary following the vision, their personal needs were met. *When we only pursue satisfying our own bag of needs, our compensation will only fill that bag.* When we pursue God's vision for our lives, there will be multiplication and eventual abundance.

If I see my job only as a means to pay bills, then my job and my future in that job will only be about paying my bills. If I have no vision for that job or being a blessing to my employer, then I will simply be an employee who is paying his bills. I will be driven by need, not by vision.

If I see my children as expensive distractions who must eat, be clothed, and go to school, I will be a need-driven caretaker, not a vision-driven parent. If I see my spouse as a burden to my life rather than a potential "enhancer" of my life, I will see my marriage as need-driven, not vision-driven. I'll be spitting out the seeds of God's grace, not sowing them.

Needs are real, but living to only meet needs is the shallowest form of life. It is not the "abundant life" that Jesus promised (see John 10:10). *The future that is possible for our lives can only be the product of spiritual vision.* A need-driven life lives for the present and perhaps a limited future. A vision-driven life sees the unseen, understands the seeds of God's grace, and expects a harvest of blessings.

How do you tell the difference between a vision and a need?

A VISION
stimulates sowing.

A diligent farmer has a vision of the harvest his seeds will bring. A parent has a vision of successful, God-loving children. A motivated athlete has a vision of playing in the big game. The vision motivates them to train continually. When there is a vision, there will be sowing toward that vision. Sowing time, patience, love, activities, words of encouragement, resources, etc. all reveal a vision.

A NEED
stimulates hoarding.

When we live only for meeting needs, we feel limited and are unwilling to give. Our job is a necessary evil, our kids are distractions, and our money is never enough. Need-driven living is ultimately self-centered, not vision-centered.

A VISION
activates faith.

Visions create energy. Faith is energy in action. Faith sees the unseen and believes it is possible. A farmer sees his seeds and projects a harvest of crops. Faith sees the seeds of God's grace and projects a harvest of blessings. A vision of a possibility will generate focus and action. A vision of a promise of God should do the same. Passivity is a symptom of not having a vision.

A NEED
activates worry.

Those who live to meet needs are always worried, anxious, and happy when the day is over. The future is seen with dread, not excitement.

A VISION
includes blessing others.

Those who live with vision are always including others in their vision. Giving, sharing, encouraging, and lifting up others are the earmarks of the visionary.

A NEED
is all about you.

A life lived to meet needs will always focus on what you've done in your own strength and how there is little time for others.

A VISION
creates positive expectation for the future.

The visionary expects the blessings of God. A visionary can "see" the promises of God and lives in the joy of knowing God's heart of love and grace.

A NEED
creates dread of the future.

"If I don't have enough now, how will I ever have enough tomorrow?" Those who live by needs will always have an inventory of needs and not of possibilities.

A VISION
ties us to the future.

A visionary anticipates the harvest of good things from the seeds of love, joy, patience, and giving that are being sown. The future is always in the heart of the visionary.

A NEED
ties us to the present.

Those who are need-driven live only in the present.

A VISION
unlocks the power of the seed.

A visionary sees the potential of what is at hand. Seeds of life-giving words, seeds of love, seeds of time, seeds of perseverance, discipline, and generosity are all sown in faith.

A NEED
harnesses the lack of the present.

Those who are need-driven will always complain about what they don't have. Though they may be Christians who carry the love and grace of God within, they cannot grasp this incredible potential and tend to see themselves as victims of circumstances.

A VISION
will keep you in the Spirit.

Living by a vision will keep you walking in the things of God. You will recognize and avoid the trap of worthless pursuits because your eyes are seeing the future.

A NEED
will tempt you in the flesh.

Living to meet needs will lead you to trust in yourself and your own strength and current resources. Living to meet needs leaves you trapped in a life of limited resources.

A VISIONARY
will stay energized.

A visionary sees possibilities, promises, and blessings. A visionary does not despise small beginnings.

THOSE DRIVEN BY NEEDS
will burn out.

A need-driven Christian will often be faithful, hardworking, dedicated, and selfless, but they will seldom unlock the potential that the visionary has discovered. They will eventually lose hope of ever getting ahead.

When you spend some time evaluating this list, it should become clear that many have spent their lives living to meet needs. In so doing, you may have missed the future that was possible. But there is grace for you! Remember, God's provision for your life was established before time began!

> *Who has saved us and called us with a holy calling, not according to our works, but according to **His own purpose and grace** which was given to us in Christ Jesus before time began* (2 Timothy 1:9).

We may have lost time, but we will never lose God's grace vision for our future. We can enter in today. The grace of God is more than enough to help us shape a new future based upon vision and not upon needs.

It's not that needs don't exist. It is how we approach them that matters. A life motivated by vision will see the needs met along the way. Don't forget that abundant life was God's

Those who are need-driven will always complain about what they don't have.

vision for you. Jesus declared His purpose for your life if you will believe it and receive it.

I have come that they may have life, and that they may have it more abundantly (John 10:10).

God's vision for you is His desire. His grace for you is His provision to see that desire realized. When we begin to recognize the potential of His life within us, we can move from the world of limitations and resignation into a world of vision, increase, and blessing.

> *We may have lost time, but we will never lose God's grace vision for our future.*

Abundance and multiplication are concepts of living by God's vision, not by your needs. In the story of the loaves and the fishes, the disciples were responding to the need and the apparent lack, while Jesus responded to a vision and the seed principle. That parable can change your life if you will let it.

A vision understands God's way of doing things. *You sow to a vision. You react to a need.* God had a vision to redeem humanity and sowed Jesus into the earth. To harvest a vision, seed must be sown. We can be talking about education, work, or even health. All future harvests begin as seeds. Those who have a vision understand the power of investing in that vision.

Within each of us there is a divine calling, gifting, and purpose. Some are so need-driven that they never even consider the seeds of God's grace in their lives.

Do you have a vision for your marriage, or was the vision simply to be married? Now what? Do you have a vision for your children, or was the vision to simply have children? Do you have a vision for your job, or do you just "need a job"? Do you have a vision for the church you attend, or do you expect the pastor to have a vision for you?

What we "see" with our spiritual eyes will create the potential for our futures. People with vision see possibilities where others see problems. *Visions are pictures of God's possibilities for your life and the lives of others based upon the seeds of His promises.*

Are you motivated to dream, to give, to serve, and to bless? You are living according to a vision.

Are you motivated to worry, fear, hoard, and complain? You are living according to your needs.

Lift up your eyes. See past the temporal and let His vision motivate you toward your divine calling and purpose. *Your future is locked in the present.* Only you can release it, sow toward it, and harvest it. Your future will follow the vision of you, the visionary.

CHAPTER 10

THE TWO TREES THAT DETERMINE OUR FUTURES

IN the Garden of Eden, God gave Adam two possible futures. Adam could eat of every tree of the garden, including the Tree of Life, or Adam could choose independence from God and eat from the Tree of the Knowledge of Good and Evil. Both trees carried distinctive futures within. God told Adam to *not* eat of the Tree of the Knowledge of Good and Evil or he would die. That is a pretty bleak future, but Adam didn't believe God. Adam chose to believe the serpent. He chose his future.

As we look at the world in which we live, it is obvious that most are still eating from the Tree of the Knowledge of Good and Evil. How can we know? We know because darkness, death, and corruption are still being harvested in ever increasing amounts. *Independence from God has a bleak future attached to it.*

The knowledge of good and evil can be understood in how we evaluate our lives and circumstances. We either "feel good" or we "feel bad." Were such feelings a gauge of how we were doing before Adam's sin? Wouldn't life in the Garden be a continual state of joy and peace? Feelings have become so important in today's culture that we are constantly worried about our own and everyone else's. Laws are being written to protect people's feelings! This is life from the Tree of the Knowledge of Good and Evil.

What about our opinions? We either like something or we don't like it. Before sin, wouldn't everything God created be good and worthy of our admiration?

We can be happy or sad. Were these emotions a part of God's creation, or are they a result of Adam's choice?

We can be healthy or sick. The sickness option did not exist before sin.

Once you start to see the reality of "good and evil," you realize that we are often still eating of the wrong tree and filling our futures with the results.

In the world of good and evil, our senses usually rule us. Our emotions need to be fed, soothed, and indulged. Our concept of right and wrong changes from generation to generation. Everything in the world of good and evil is subject to change. As a result, there is no standard of truth to which we look, and as individuals and as a society we are harvesting the corruption of Adam's sin. Futures are being determined based on feelings, emotions, and ever-changing morality. And then many will wonder, "Why did God let this happen to me?"

If we are going to shape our futures according to the goodness of God, then we must choose the Tree of Life. It alone offers the future God wants for His children. What is "life"? How can we know we are eating from that tree?

> *And this is eternal life, that they may know You, the only true God, and Jesus Christ whom You have sent* (John 17:3).

If Adam and Eve had valued knowing God over knowing good and evil, we would be living in a different world. But let's make it more personal. If we would value knowing Him over our senses, feelings, likes, dislikes, and emotions, we would harvest the abundant life and future that He desires for us.

There is a difference between truth and facts. I am going to speak of facts that are not based in eternal truth, but rather in the ever-changing, partial knowledge of our culture and society, that is, facts that come from the Tree of the Knowledge of Good and Evil. Even in the world of science, things which were facts 50 years ago are no longer facts today. In my lifetime, eggs for breakfast have been good, not good, healthy, dangerous, okay, suspect, and good again. I'm not sure what the "facts" are as I write this. I could offer many such examples of what science has declared evil and then later declared good. Or what has been a fact and now is a myth.

The same can be said for morality. What was considered a mental disorder a few decades ago is now considered normal, and those who believe that certain behaviors or lifestyles are abnormal are now classified as the ones with the problem.

A few years ago, I noticed a growth in my ear, so I went to a dermatologist to have it checked. He did a biopsy and determined it was skin cancer. He told me I would need surgery to get it all out, and due to the damage that would occur from surgery, I would then need plastic surgery. These were facts. He could scientifically show me the test results.

Many years ago, my firstborn was declared dead in the womb. I was shown the medical evidence and the doctor proclaimed, "The fetus is dead." These were facts supported by medical evidence.

I once had a large kidney stone, and after an MRI I was told that it was too large to pass normally and would have to be removed by a procedure. This was a "fact."

In each case, the Spirit of God rose up within me and declared, "NO!" There was something in me that was greater than the facts and greater than the knowledge of good and evil. Truth rose up within me, and the truth is that by His stripes I was healed (see Isa. 53:5). Truth is superior to transitory facts. But you must know the truth and it must be a foundation of your life if you are going to be able to let truth shape your future.

I was miraculously healed from skin cancer in my ear with no further medical treatment. My son was born perfectly healthy in spite of the "fact" that he was dead in the womb. The kidney stone passed with no pain two days after the verdict from the doctor. Truth will always be superior to the facts the world has to offer. *The future you desire is a product of truth, not the world's facts.* Jesus spoke to this incredible revelation:

If you abide in My word, you are My disciples indeed. And you shall know the truth, and the truth shall make you free (John 8:31-32)

Only God's truth can make you free. The Tree of Life was a tree of truth, not ever-changing facts and opinions. So many are in bondage today because their source for the future offers no freedom at all.

I encourage you to stop and meditate on this verse and the contents of this chapter. Your future is contained in two trees. The tree you choose to eat from is what will be in your heart, and as we have seen, out of your heart springs your future.

Truth is the knowledge of God, the Tree of Life. *"And this is eternal life, that they may know You"* (John 17:3).

We are either living our lives according to the Tree of Life, which is the knowledge of God, or the Tree of the Knowledge of Good and Evil, which is the world of our senses, emotions, and "facts." The knowledge and application of God's truth is a potential future. It is a future filled with life, peace, joy, and increase. Living in the world of "good and evil" will never unlock the promises of God. It will keep you trapped in the cycle of loss, sickness, and lack.

The foundation on which we have built our lives will determine the potential of the future. So many well-meaning Christians live in the world of good and evil, feelings, emotions, and facts. They even relate to God as Job did. "The Lord gives and the Lord takes away" is a perfect example of eating from the wrong tree. Can you see the problem? Job later repented of his ignorance (see Job 42:1-6).

Consider the reaction of Adam and Eve once they ate of the Tree of the Knowledge of Good and Evil. Let's look at the results that continue to impact all of us on a daily basis.

> *Then the eyes of both of them were opened, and they knew that they were naked; and they sewed fig leaves together and made themselves coverings. And they heard the sound of the Lord God walking in the garden in the cool of the day, and Adam and his wife hid themselves from the presence of the Lord God among the trees of the garden. Then the Lord God called to Adam and said to him, "Where are you?" So he said, "I heard Your voice in the garden, and I was afraid because I was naked; and I hid myself." And He said, "Who told you that you were naked? Have you eaten from the tree of which I commanded you that you should not eat?" Then the man said, "The woman whom You gave to be with me, she gave me of the tree, and I ate"* (Genesis 3:7-12).

Let's go through this passage and look at the various concepts that are revealed. If you are really interested in your future, you should pay attention.

Then the eyes of both of them were opened.

What were they seeing before? They saw the Garden. They saw the trees. They saw the serpent. They saw each other. In what way were their eyes opened? After eating of the Tree of the Knowledge of Good and Evil, they began to see with natural, carnal eyes that viewed things as either good or evil. Nothing really changed but their perception.

> **They sewed fig leaves together and made themselves coverings.**

Their new vision or perception of evil created the need for covering their nakedness. They had been naked before (perhaps their bodies shone with the glory of the Lord and now that glory had departed), but now their perception of evil required a "work" to cover it.

> *And they heard the sound of the Lord God walk-*
> *ing in the garden in the cool of the day, and Adam*
> *and his wife hid themselves from the presence of*
> *the Lord God.*

Communion between God and man was at the heart of God's creation. He made man in His image in order to have fellowship on a level that was impossible with angels and animals. The sound of God's voice should have been the most stimulating, joy-producing, and peace-giving sound ever. But because of their perception of good and evil, Adam and Eve hid themselves. This is mind boggling. God hadn't changed. *But the knowledge of good and evil had changed their perception of God.* That confused perception remains to this day and, sadly, is a part of many theologies in the church.

> "I heard Your voice in the garden,
> and I was afraid because I was naked;
> and I hid myself."

Fear entered the human race, and sadly it began with fear of God Himself. *Living according to the knowledge of good and evil will always distort your image of God.* All human fears were birthed from the first fear in the Garden. Just as the truth will make us free, the lies of the knowledge of good and evil will make us slaves to fear.

> Then the man said, "The woman whom
> You gave to be with me, she gave me
> of the tree, and I ate."

This would be funny if it wasn't so sad. The knowledge of good and evil immediately created the need to deal with guilt. Besides sewing fig leaves, Adam felt the need to blame someone else for his mistake. Deflecting blame for our mistakes and failures is a common trait of living from the wrong tree. And what is incredible is that Adam not only blamed Eve, but he also blamed God. "It was this woman's fault, *and You gave her to me.*" Do you see it? Adam's guilt needed someone to blame, and who better to blame than God! And many are still blaming God today. The clichés I discussed earlier in this book are simply various ways of blaming God. They are symptoms of the knowledge of good and evil.

Once we become aware of our unconscious dependence on "good and evil" for the way we live, it can be shocking. It explains why so many are living in difficult and dramatic situations with little hope for a better future. *There is no future of blessing in the Tree of the Knowledge of Good and Evil.*

The future that God has in His heart for His children will never be built on the "facts" of the world or the knowledge of good and evil. His future for your life will only come from a foundation of life and truth. Jesus declared that He was the only way, truth, and life.

> *Jesus said to him, "I am the way, the truth, and the life. No one comes to the Father except through Me"* (John 14:6).

He is now the Tree of Life for all who will believe and receive Him. Coming to the Father includes coming into the abundant life and potential that God had purposed for us from before time began.

Living according to the knowledge of good and evil will always distort your image of God.

Until His truth is alive in our hearts, we will continue to indulge our feelings, emotions, likes, dislikes, and the ever-changing facts all around us. A Christian may be born again and have the Spirit of God living within, but if that Christian doesn't live from the Spirit, his future is limited to what the world offers. And the world will always offer the two-edged sword of good and evil. There is no life in that tree, only the roller coaster of natural living in a fallen world.

LET GO OF THE POPCORN

Before moving to Chile where we spent many years as missionaries, we spent ten months in Huehuetenango, Guatemala to study Spanish. Our lives there were more "rustic" and filled with new things. It was an adventure we will never forget.

One day when returning from a long walk to the market, we entered our home and I immediately saw something moving on the floor. I moved closer and saw that a piece of popcorn was on the floor. I love popcorn. This piece had apparently escaped my last feeding frenzy. However, the popcorn was moving. It was actually spinning in circles. I had never seen spinning popcorn before, so I bent over to get a better look. I saw an incredible scene of five tiny ants, all one behind the other, carrying the popcorn while a sixth ant was standing on top. I could imagine that the ant on top was the leader, and in his tiny ant voice was shouting instructions and encouragement to the ants working below him. "Keep it up guys, you're doing great!" "We're making good time!" But what the ants failed to realize is that for all their effort, they were going in circles. Each ant was following the ant in front, and the result was a lot of ant energy spent and no progress toward the goal. I sent the whole group to ant heaven, and then took some time to think about the moral of the story.

How many live their lives going in circles? They are fulfilling the principles of effort, teamwork, and submission to authority, but they are going nowhere. Their future is limited.

Someone needs to let go of the popcorn and take a look around.

God's heart for your future is not an endless cycle of circles. Think of the man lying at the pool of Bethesda in John 5. He had been there for 38 years! Was that the future that God had for him, or was he simply holding on to the popcorn because that was all he knew?

Think of blind Bartimaeus who had been a blind beggar his entire life. Was that all that God had for him? What changed his future?

God who lives within you is a changer of futures! Remember that God had a purpose and grace for you from before time began:

> [He] *has saved us and called us with a holy calling, not according to our works, but according to **His own purpose and grace which was given to us in Christ Jesus before time began*** (2 Timothy 1:9).

Even when we think we are doing everything right, we may be missing God's purpose for our lives. When I was growing up it was considered normal and right to go to college after high school. I didn't have a vision for college, and once there I quickly lost my way due to all of the influences around me. But I was convinced that this was what was expected in order to be successful in life. It was my "popcorn" for the future.

I came to a place of frustration and began to search for a deeper meaning for my life. It was early in my third year of college that I was born again and began to discover a more eternal purpose for my life. My future changed the moment I ate from the Tree of Life (Jesus). I didn't instantly know then what I know now, but my pursuit of things eternal has unfolded into a life of purpose and blessing.

I am not suggesting that all routine is bad. I am a person who enjoys routine. I am more productive with routine. But my routine has been shaped by letting go of the popcorn of human expectation many times over the years.

Leaving college in my senior year may have seemed foolish, but I knew my future was no longer tied to that "popcorn." When I enrolled in Bible college, I had very little money. It was not the routine I would have preferred. Getting married while in Bible college when I only had a part-time job was a giant step of faith for my wife. Going to Mexico as hopeful missionaries after having been married only eight months was a major life lesson. Taking my family of five to Guatemala and Chile for twelve and a half years was no normal routine. Was everything perfect and without challenges in each of those seasons? No. But as I look back from my current vantage point, I can see that I was eating from the Tree of Life. I was pursuing God more than I was satisfied with the knowledge of good and evil, logic, human wisdom, and "safety." The future of that 20-year-old college kid is now my past, but I was allowing God to give me something I would have never received if I hadn't let go of the popcorn of cultural routine.

Today, by God's grace, I have influence through Charis Bible College and Andrew Wommack Ministries that goes around the world. My present was only made possible by not settling for the Tree of the Knowledge of Good and Evil but rather choosing the Tree of Life.

As we begin to substitute God's truth for the world's facts, we are laying a foundation for building our lives. Truth is the unchanging nature of God. Truth is found in the words that come from His mouth. Truth is the person of Jesus. Truth includes the benefits of redemption and all the promises of God. Truth is the only foundation for a future of blessing.

> *Truth is the only foundation for a future of blessing.*

Health flows from the truth that by His stripes you were healed (see 1 Pet. 2:24). True love flows from God's truth concerning marriage and sexual intimacy. Peace and joy flow from the truth of knowing God. Faith flows from hearing God. Authority over the enemy flows from our new identity in Him.

Everything that men and women want, and may not even know that they want, comes from the Tree of Life. The Tree of the Knowledge of Good and Evil has carried us to where we are today, with a world full of mental illness, sickness, poverty, injustice, war, crime, confusion, and heartache. It carries a future of pain, bitterness, and anger. We see it on the news every day.

You can take charge of your future if you are willing to. There is grace for you to cooperate with God's purpose for your life. You don't have to be a missionary like I was. You are free to live the dream that God put in your heart from before time began! It is possible that some of you reading this book may not have even found the dream yet. The knowledge of good and evil has hidden the Tree of Life. But it is still there in the person of Jesus. You can begin your new future today.

CHAPTER 11

THE GRACE
IS IN THE SEED!

WHEN we speak of the future, it is important that we see it as something greater than just our own personal fulfillment. Farmers don't plant their seeds just for themselves. When you are walking in God's grace and purpose for your life, it will always involve blessing others. That is God's heart. God loves the world, so He sowed a Seed, Jesus. His vision was to have a family. The possibility of God having a family was locked into the person of Jesus. The future of humanity was contained in a divine Seed, Jesus.

As a husband, my vision is to bless my wife. As a father my vision is to bless my children and now my grandchildren. As a teacher my vision is to bless thousands of people around the world. In blessing others (sowing), I reap. I am reaping health and prosperity (mental, emotional, relational, physical, and spiritual prosperity). I live free from fear and depression. I enjoy life and I am looking forward to an even more blessed future. But my harvest of the present has everything to do with my seeds of the past. I chose to "let go of the popcorn" of the world's way of doing things and invest my life in sowing into others.

In the process I have discovered grace. Grace is a word that few understand, but it has everything to do with the future God wants you to have.

What is grace? We can find a great definition of grace in 2 Corinthians 9.

> *And God is able to make all grace abound toward you, that you, **always having all sufficiency in all things, may have an abundance for every good work*** (2 Corinthians 9:8).

When you are walking in God's grace and purpose for your life, it will always involve blessing others.

Always having all sufficiency in all things and an abundance for good works is grace. I like to call God's grace His provision for every human need—spirit, soul, and body. There is no human need that exceeds God's provision. *Grace is God's provision for your present and your future.* Whatever Adam's sin unleashed into the world, the abundant solution has been provided for by God's grace. John describes grace as an opposing force to the law of works.

And of His fullness we have all received, and grace for grace. For

*the law was given through Moses, **but grace and
truth came through Jesus Christ** (John 1:16-17).*

*The Law of Moses was the pinnacle of the knowledge of
good and evil.* The Law solved nothing but made man's need
very apparent. The Law did not provide for man's need; it
simply revealed it. In contrast, grace is God's provision for
man. Grace is the supply of God's love, forgiveness, peace,
joy, faith, healing, prosperity, and abundance. Jesus brought
grace (provision) and truth (that sets us free) in order to give
us a future.

So where does grace come from and how do we tap into it?
Let's think about seeds again.

As we have discussed, the Word of God is a seed and our
words are seeds. Paul spoke of the word of His grace, which
is able to build us up and give us an inheritance. The gospel
is "the word of His grace."

> *And now, brethren, I commend you to God, and to
> **the word of his grace**, which is able to build you
> up, and to give you an inheritance among all them
> which are sanctified* (Acts 20:32 KJV).

Jesus referred to His words as seeds (see Matt. 13:23).
Jesus Himself was the Seed that fell into the earth and died.

> *But Jesus answered them, saying, "The hour has
> come that the Son of Man should be glorified. Most
> assuredly, I say to you, unless a grain of wheat falls
> into the ground and dies, it remains alone; but if it
> dies, it produces much grain"* (John 12:23-24).

The glory of a seed is its fruit or flower after having grown from the earth. Jesus's glory was revealed in His resurrection. Jesus's resurrection and glorification has brought forth the harvest of believers for the past 2,000 years. We are the harvest from that Seed!

The Seed, Jesus, came full of grace and truth.

> *And the Word became flesh and dwelt among us, and we beheld His glory, the glory as of the only begotten of the Father, **full of grace and truth*** (John 1:14).

We have discussed how the future of the earth and of mankind was all contained in creation in seed form, and it was "very good." The grace or provision for abundance, multiplication, and potential was all programmed into the seeds of creation. The seeds were revealing the invisible attributes of God through what has been made (see Rom. 1:20).

In every seed there is a potential destiny or purpose. *A seed is filled with "tomorrows."* A seed is packed with a purpose. A flower seed is purposed to produce a flower. A healing promise is purposed to produce a healing. Every seed will reproduce according to the nature of its purpose. In every seed there exists the potential for unlimited harvests that contain uncountable seeds.

When we understand that grace is God's provision for mankind's every need, then we can see clearly that God's grace for man's natural needs *is in the seeds* that He created in the beginning, and God's grace for man's spiritual, emotional, mental, and physical needs is contained in the Seed, Jesus.

Now read John 1:14 again. Jesus, the Seed of redemption (God in the flesh), came full of…grace and truth.

> *And the Word became flesh and dwelt among us, and we beheld His glory, the glory as of the only begotten of the Father, **full of grace and truth** (John 1:14).*

Your future from God is in the Seed of God's grace, Jesus.

The grace of God for mankind—that is, His love, provision, forgiveness, faith, nature, peace, joy, authority, and promises—all came in the Seed, Jesus. *The grace of God is in the seed.* Your future from God is in the Seed of God's grace, Jesus.

There is enough grace in Jesus to redeem every person on earth, to heal them, to provide for them, and to reveal to them the purpose that was planned for them from before time began! Think of that. The answer to all the problems in this world came packaged in the person of Jesus. The grace of God came as a Seed.

> *Who has saved us and called us with a holy calling, not according to our works, but according to **His own purpose and grace** which was given to us **in Christ Jesus** before time began (2 Timothy 1:9).*

God planned your redemption, your purpose, and your blessed life before He created anything. Provision for you to escape the consequences of Adam's sin was packaged in the Seed, Christ. Provision was made for your peace, joy, health,

153

and abundance. Your future was packaged into creation and then redeemed from sin through the Seed, Jesus. And now you have been born again by the Seed that is filled with the grace and truth to give you a future. Your true future begins in Jesus, the Seed of God's Word made flesh.

> *Having been born again, not of corruptible seed but incorruptible, through the word of God which lives and abides forever* (1 Peter 1:23).

Do you see it? Your potential future is contained in an incorruptible seed, the Word of God, which lives and abides forever. Every need you have and every vision God has for you is all provided for through Jesus.

The Word of God is the incorruptible seed that comes packed with God's grace for your future, your purpose, your health, your prosperity, and your vision.

If you can grasp this, it will fill in all the blanks in your theology. God's grace for your life begins in Jesus and flows from the seeds of His words.

Every seed bears the nature of its source. A watermelon seed bears the nature of the watermelon it came from. We can trace that nature all the way back to creation. There are no watermelons that go beyond the original nature that God made possible in the beginning.

The incorruptible seed of God's Word by which we are born again carries the nature of its Source, God Himself! *Every believer carries the "image of God" on the inside.* There are no inferior editions in the Kingdom. All who are born again carry the same nature of God that was revealed in

Jesus. And Jesus, the Word made flesh, declared, *"The words that I speak to you are spirit, and they are life"* (John 6:63).

In other words, when the Word (Jesus) speaks, His words carry His Spirit and His life. His words carry His grace and truth. *His words are the seeds of His grace.* As we hear and receive these grace seeds, they will bear fruit in our lives. We could think of the gospel as a limitless bag of grace seeds, each seed fully prepared to accomplish God's purpose in your life.

I often hear Christians wishing that they had lived during the days of Jesus or in the time of the book of Acts. They feel that back then there was power, but now we are barely getting by. "Why can't we see the same power as they did in the book of Acts?"

It can be compared to the old copy machines that were around before the digital age. A copy of a copy would produce a slightly inferior version of the original. If we were to continue to make copies of copies, each copy would be less precise. We would eventually have a very fuzzy copy of the original.

Many Christians see themselves as fuzzy copies of the early Christians. But that isn't true. The same incorruptible seed that got the first Christians born again got us born again. The seed doesn't diminish in potential and purpose. It is eternal and carries the nature of the Source. God's Word hasn't lost its life-giving, transforming power. But perhaps we have lost faith in God's Word and failed to understand the power of the grace that is in the seed.

The story of the two farmers mentioned earlier in this book is a story of grace received and grace rejected. Grace made the provision of land, house, equipment, and seeds. One farmer saw the potential of the "grace" he had received while the other farmer assumed that if the provision had been given, the harvest would be given as well. The vision of each farmer determined the future of the grace. One farmer didn't receive a lesser version of provision than the other farmer. The provision was the same, but their visions were different. The farmer who relaxed and didn't put his "grace" to work came up empty.

How can we see a multiplication of His grace (His abundant provision) in our lives? Peter declared, "*Grace and peace be multiplied unto you through the knowledge of God, and of Jesus our Lord*" (2 Pet. 1:2 KJV). *Knowing God multiplies grace in our lives.* The more we know Him, His nature, His love, His power, and His purposes, the more His grace seeds spring up in our lives. Grace and peace are multiplied in our lives through knowledge just as natural seeds produce a harvest for the farmer. And that grace carries your future possibilities. But remember, you are the visionary. There is more than enough, but you determine how far God's grace will go in your life.

All of His seeds are alive and active and ready to go to work!

> *For all the promises of God in Him are Yes, and in Him Amen, to the glory of God through us* (2 Corinthians 1:20).

Every promise carries within the power to be fulfilled. The only requirement is that the seed of that promise find the good soil of your heart. There is no need for lack in our lives.

Those who live with lack haven't yet understood the power of the seeds of grace. There is no need to lack joy, peace, love and faith, vision and purpose. Your future will follow your vision for the seeds of grace God has given you.

The seeds of His grace are abundant. Jesus clearly described how the Kingdom works by using the truth I am discussing in this book. The Kingdom is all about seed, sowing, and reaping.

> *And He said, "The kingdom of God is as if a man should scatter seed on the ground, and should sleep by night and rise by day, and the seed should sprout and grow, he himself does not know how. For the earth yields crops by itself: first the blade, then the head, after that the full grain in the head"* (Mark 4:26-28).

Your heart is the soil that transforms the seed into a harvest. Out of the abundance of your heart comes your future. This is how the Kingdom works.

One word from God can change your future forever! It carries God's grace.

When we first moved to Colorado to hopefully become a part of Andrew Wommack's ministry, no one knew us. I had a word from God and believed that God had a place for us in this ministry. By God's grace I was offered a position in the phone center, praying for those who called in with various needs. I was happy to do so. I had been a missionary in Latin America, a pastor, and the director of a Spanish Bible school in Dallas, but I sensed God's grace and purpose for me in simply praying for people over the phone.

About a year and a half later, while driving to work with my wife who also was working in Andrew's ministry, we were at a traffic light and my cell phone rang. My boss from the phone center was calling and said that the Bible college administrator (both the ministry headquarters and the Bible college were in the same building at the time) was standing next to him asking if I would be willing to preach a chapel session to the students at 8 A.M. It was 7:50 A.M. when I got the call. I was in my car still five minutes away from the building.

The word from God that I had received two years earlier was that one day I would teach at Charis Bible College. No one knew about that. I had no idea how it would come to pass. And now, in the car at a traffic light I am being asked to preach in ten minutes! I heard the Lord say, "Tell them yes." I thought, "I am not prepared! What will I speak on for 50 minutes?" I responded to my boss with a bit of false confidence, "Sure, I'd love to." It was time to receive God's grace!

The moment I arrived at the building, I ran into my office, grabbed my notes from my Spanish Bible college curriculum (before moving to Colorado, I had been ministering for 18 years in Spanish, but not English), found a message I felt I could do on the spur of the moment, and ran into the auditorium. Would there be grace (provision) for me?

The students didn't know me, but I proceeded to minister in English from my Spanish notes, and it seemed to go well. Without going into more of the story, I have been teaching in Charis Bible College ever since and now teach 16 courses, speak in conferences, and have traveled to a number of countries teaching and preaching. The videos of my teachings go around the world. God's grace has been more than enough.

But it began with the seed of a promise, the "harvest" of a phone call, and the faith to say "yes." My future was changed by a phone call and God's grace.

Friends, *the grace of God for your future is in the seeds of His promises.* You have no idea what the possibilities are until you believe and receive His Word. You can shape your future with God's grace seeds.

Put His grace seeds (His Word, His promises, and the knowledge of God) to work in your life. There is more than enough for all of us! Your future is in the seeds that you are sowing. Decide to sow the seeds (promises) of His grace into your life, your marriage, your children, your job, and your ministry. Choose to see what God sees and sow toward it. *His grace is in the seeds.*

The harvest of God's grace contains within it the potential to touch and transform the world. The seed of grace is meant to be sown in order to create multiplication and continuing harvests. If we only partake of the harvest for ourselves, that potential will remain untapped. I can enjoy a watermelon and even share some with my friends. That is one level of grace (provision.) But if I throw away the seeds, the "grace" contained for future watermelons is wasted. Paul speaks of wasted grace in his letter to the Corinthians:

> *We then, as workers together with Him also plead with you not to receive the grace of God in vain* (2 Corinthians 6:1).

While there is a contextual application to Paul's words in this verse, there is also a conceptual application. Harvesting

God's blessings in our lives without considering the possibility of seeing those blessings multiply to bless others is short sighted. In such cases we have received God's grace in vain. There is bread for the eater *and* seed for the sower in the grace of God (see 2 Cor. 9:10-11).

God forgiving you isn't just about you. It is also about you forgiving others.

> *And be kind to one another, tenderhearted, forgiving one another, even as God in Christ forgave you* (Ephesians 4:32).

The grace that forgave you is now in you to forgive others.

The grace that heals you is now in you to bring healing to others. The grace that gives you peace is now in you so that you can sow peace in others. When you are born again by the seed of God's Word, every aspect of God's original intention for humanity is in you in seed form. It is for you, and it is for you to sow into those around you. Paul understood that grace not only provides for you, but also is destined to bring abundance to others. You simply need a vision.

Sowing brings a harvest, and in the harvest there is the seed for future sowing. In every harvest are the seeds for the future.

> *Now may He who supplies seed to the sower, and bread for food, supply and multiply the seed you have sown and* **increase the fruits of your righteousness** (2 Corinthians 9:10).

You have harvested the gift of righteousness by God's grace. In the fruit of righteousness is a seed that can change families, churches, workplaces, communities, and even nations. When we sow the seeds of righteousness, we increase the "fruits of righteousness." In other words, lives and destinies can be changed if we would allow the grace in us to touch those around us.

How big is God's grace? Let me put it to you this way. *If you were the only person on earth who was born again, there is enough of God's grace in that incorruptible seed within you to bring salvation and healing to everyone alive.* One seed can do that!

When I saw that truth, my own challenges became much smaller in my heart. If there is enough of God's grace in me to bring His saving and healing power to the world, there is enough to overcome the challenges of my own life.

Do you have a revelation of what lives in you? Your future and the future of many others is in the seed of His word that is alive in your heart. You can shape the future by unlocking the seeds of God's grace.

CHAPTER 12

DISCOVERING YOUR PURPOSE

HAVE you ever wondered why you are on this earth? Many live frustrated lives and often wonder why they are alive. What possible purpose could they have? Discovering our purpose is an adventure available to us all if we have some basic understanding.

God has a purpose for our lives that He established before time began. Paul reminded us of this fact when he wrote to Timothy:

> *Who has saved us and called us with a holy calling, not according to our works, but **according to His own purpose and grace which was given to us in Christ Jesus before time began**, but has now been revealed by the appearing of our Savior Jesus Christ, who has abolished death and brought life and immortality to light through the gospel* (2 Timothy 1:9-10).

What is the purpose and grace which was given to you? Just as with the watermelon seed, we are the ones who establish how far we will allow God's grace and purpose to flow through our lives. God's ultimate purpose for us all is that we have abundant lives that reflect His love and bless others (see John 10:10). His more specific purpose for us as individuals will be a process of growth and discovery. The grace is in us if we are born again, but will we choose to discover it?

Let's consider the story of Abram/Abraham as a key to understanding how to discover God's purpose for your life. God's instructions to Abraham when He called him reveal a tremendous amount about how we can discover God's purpose for our lives and, by extension, enter into the future that will bless us and those around us.

> *Now the Lord had said to Abram: "Get out of your country, from your family and from your father's house, to a land that I will show you. I will make you a great nation; I will bless you and make your name great; and you shall be a blessing"* (Genesis 12:1-2).

As I was reading this passage years ago, I noticed a sequence of events that I believe reveals how to shape our futures and be a blessing in the world in which we live. We are going to look at six concepts revealed in this passage.

1. Separation

2. Vision

3. Formation

4. Increase

5. Influence

6. Being a blessing

Let's break this down one concept at a time.

SEPARATION

"Get out of your country, from your family and from your father's house." Before God would be able to lead Abram (Abraham) into the future He had purposed for him, *there had to be a separation from his past and present.* God's intentions for Abraham would not be realized until Abraham was no longer under the influence of all that had shaped him up until this point in his life.

In our understanding as Christians, we could see this as the "new birth" and our decision to follow Christ. Being born again is by nature a separation from our old life and a decision to walk in "newness of life." This is one of the reasons Paul writes:

> *Therefore we are buried with him by baptism into death: that like as Christ was raised up from the dead by the glory of the Father, even so **we also should walk in newness of life*** (Romans 6:4 KJV).

Have you made a break with the past and the influences of the present? Not necessarily a geographical break, but a tangible decision in your heart to separate from the things that have held you back and be fully committed to walking with God? The writer of Hebrews puts it this way:

> *Therefore we also, since we are surrounded by so great a cloud of witnesses, **let us lay aside every weight, and the sin which so easily ensnares us**, and let us run with endurance the race that is set before us, looking unto Jesus, the author and finisher of our faith* (Hebrews 12:1-2).

Many never realize their purpose or shape their futures because their hearts have never separated from the world. John realized the temptations that the world offers and the dangers involved.

> *Do not love the world or the things in the world. If anyone loves the world, the love of the Father is not in him. For all that is in the world—the lust of the flesh, the lust of the eyes, and the pride of life—is not of the Father but is of the world. And the world is passing away, and the lust of it; but he who does the will of God abides forever* (1 John 2:15-17).

While we still live in the world, our love cannot be for the world. To the degree that we want the world's approval or we are enticed to live as worldly people live, the separation that is necessary for shaping our futures is diminished. I am not speaking of a geographical separation (though that can be necessary in some cases), but more importantly a heart separation from the things that have entangled us in the past and shaped our lives up until now. Your present was shaped by your past. Will the future be any different? Only if you choose to separate your heart unto Him who desires an abundant future for you.

As a young college student, when introduced to the message of the gospel, I was very hesitant to give up some of the new things I was experiencing. For two years I was unwilling to separate from those influences. My future was blocked by my unwilling heart. It was only when I saw that my true future of purpose and blessing would come from Him that I was willing to separate from the temporal pursuits of a typical 20-year-old college student.

Separating from the influences of friends and family does not mean we become rude or unloving, but rather that we see those people through God's eyes and recognize that we cannot be bound by any influence that would keep us in the realm of darkness. When we are separated unto God, we are by default separating from the influences that have shaped us before knowing Jesus.

I understand that this is going to be perceived differently by different readers, and I want to be very careful with my words. I am not advocating divorcing a spouse, quitting a job, or living in the mountains as a hermit. I am simply saying that in order for God's grace and purpose to prosper in our lives, that grace and purpose must be more important to us than worldly endeavors that do not give life.

For those who are married, the separation is unto God, not away from a spouse. You are in a covenant relationship that God has ordained, even if your spouse is not a believer. In fact, that relationship has much more potential once you are separated unto God and can now love your spouse with the love of God. The same holds true for our relationships with parents and friends. Our separation unto God makes us more relevant to them as ambassadors of the gospel rather than prisoners of their possible ungodly influence.

It is possible to honor your father and mother while at the same time cutting the cords of their influence in order to follow God's will for your life. A separation in your heart is not an excuse for unloving behavior. It is simply seeing your life from a different dimension and being willing to pursue the things of God from a place of freedom without soulish bondage.

My parents loved me deeply but struggled to understand my walk with the Lord. While I honored them and wanted to please them, I knew my path would take me into a life they were unfamiliar with. It was years later that they began to understand and appreciate the decisions I had made. While the separation was difficult at the time, the grace of God was more than enough to keep our relationships strong. Toward the ends of their lives they both expressed positive feelings about me, my family, and my life of ministry.

VISION

Next, God told Abraham, *"Get out of your country, from your family and from your father's house, **to a land that I will show you.**"* The second part of our journey into the future involves vision. Notice that what God would show to Abraham would only happen *after* Abraham was separated from his country (his old way of living). God's vision for our futures cannot be fully revealed while we are still attracted to our old lives. *Vision follows separation.* To the degree that we embrace our old lives, we are limiting God's vision for our futures. When separation unto Him is complete, the future begins to become clearer, much as when a morning fog lifts to reveal a spectacular landscape.

Vision is an interesting subject. I am not speaking of supernatural dreams and visions at this point, but rather the vision of the heart. In my own experience, my vision for my future has evolved over time. In fact, I find myself at the time of this writing working for a ministry I didn't know existed when we returned from the mission field in 2001. The vision isn't always about the circumstances or people we know, but rather about understanding the grace gift that is in us. Let me explain.

As a missionary in Chile, I began to discover and develop in the grace of teaching that God had put in me "before time began." I was not always aware of that grace, but as a missionary and pastor I began to realize that teaching, writing, and communicating were my true passions. My years of Spanish ministry helped me grow in that gift. Our futures have much more to do with discovering our grace and purpose than they do with being in a certain place with a certain job or title. *Places, jobs, and titles come and go, but purpose and grace remain.* Doors will open and circumstances will change if we are walking in our purpose and grace. The future is more about what God has placed within us than where we are geographically.

Vision follows separation. While I was dedicated to serving the Lord and His people in Chile, the vision of writing and teaching grew and grew. Had I not remained separated unto God, no doubt my current circumstances would not have happened.

When I drive home from a nighttime meeting or class, I cannot see my house from where I am parked. If I refuse to drive until I can see my house, I would never leave the parking lot. I must drive in the light of the headlights, and as I do, I can see a little farther with each rotation of the tires. I won't see my house until I am just a few yards away, but I was able to arrive because I drove in the light I had available.

> *Being a blessing now is the key to the door of the future.*

So it is with our lives. We can't see our futures with the details of circumstances, people, and places, but we can see what is next and how to be a blessing where we are. As we walk in the grace that we have for the present, the future becomes clearer. Vision has so much to do with our hearts for where we are. Being a blessing now is the key to the door of the future.

What is next in our journey into the future? Let's return to the story of Abram (Abraham).

FORMATION

"I will make you a great nation," God told Abraham. As we continue to look at God's call to Abraham, we come to this interesting declaration. It is actually this short sentence that

gave birth to all that I am sharing in this chapter. As I read this many years ago, the words *I will make you* jumped off the page. I saw in my heart God's heart to shape our futures and bless our lives. He wants to be intimately involved in our lives and give shape to the purpose that is in us. This is not a controlling force, but rather a divine cooperation with those who are separated unto Him and who see the possibilities to bless others.

Discovering our purpose is a lifelong process. When I teach on discovering our purpose in Bible college, I refer to life as something of a triangle. We enter at the broad base of the triangle when we are born again, and there we find so many opportunities to serve and bless others. In my own life I have been involved in many different kinds of ministries and services for others. From street evangelism to jail ministry, to home groups, to a ministry to Cambodian refugees in Dallas, to serving on various committees in churches, we have made ourselves available. In our earliest years in Chile, I began by helping the little church we were serving by making oatmeal for underprivileged children several mornings a week. I did puppet shows, led worship in Spanish, and finally began teaching as there were opportunities.

The base of the "triangle of life" is broad, and I encourage young Christians to get involved in serving and blessing others as much as they can. It is in the experiences of serving that we begin to discover our passion and that which truly blesses others. As the years go by, the sides of the triangle narrow. We are learning where our gifts are most effective and perhaps leaving some kinds of service behind. I no longer do puppets and jail ministry, but it doesn't mean I couldn't. I've simply discovered where I am most effective. In this season of my life, I am at the top of the triangle of discovery and have developed the grace and purpose that God placed in me before time began. Time was lost here and there through mistakes and hardness of heart, but God's grace and purpose never diminished. God's heart was to "make of Abraham a great nation," but it was Abraham who had to cooperate. God will not force a destiny on you that you have no interest in.

The writer of Hebrews reveals that Abraham was aware of God's call but could either follow the call or stay where he was.

> *God will not force a destiny on you that you have no interest in.*

By faith Abraham obeyed when he was called to go out to *the place which he would receive as an inheritance. And he went out, not knowing where he was going* (Hebrews 11:8).

God made of Abraham a great nation, but it was Abraham who obeyed and agreed to discover what his destiny would look like.

INCREASE

Allowing God to bring shape to our lives unlocks the next part of the journey. The blessing of God follows the heart that is submitted to His heart.

> *I will make you a great nation;* **I will bless you**
> (Genesis 12:2).

In the sequence of events that led Abraham into his future, we find God's declaration that He would bless Abraham. As I considered this, I realized that *the blessing followed the separation, vision, and willingness to pursue that which God had purposed.* In other words, there is provision and increase when we are walking in our purpose.

So many Christians seem to lack God's provision in their lives and are stuck in their growth. We often become settled and even passive at some point and, rather than expecting an ever-increasing walk with God filled with purpose and blessing, we learn to make do. Jesus spoke along these lines when He declared:

> *I am the vine, you are the branches. He who abides in Me, and I in him, bears much fruit; for without Me you can do nothing* (John 15:5).

Dependence on our fellowship with God through Jesus is the source of life, purpose, vision, and increase. Independence leaves us in our own strength and stalled in life. Without Him we can do nothing. His blessing (much fruit) follows those who abide in Him.

When God spoke His promise and intention to Abraham, the blessing was contingent upon 1) the heart separation from his present and past, 2) his new vision for the future, and 3) his willingness to discover God's purpose for his life. God's provision and increase followed God's purpose.

When I speak of God's increase and provision, I am not speaking only of a bank account. I am speaking of favor, opportunities, health, joy, peace, and love. The future of every person on this earth was provided for in those areas. That is the grace and purpose that existed in the heart of God for you before time began (see 2 Tim. 1:9). God's heart for Abraham was that he be the father of many nations, the vessel through whom He would bring forth the Promise for mankind, Jesus. Abraham's obedience to the call unleashed the grace of God's increase.

Your future and mine remain in front of us. Wherever we are in life at this moment, the future can be better. Our heart separation unto Him and our willingness to discover His ways will bring the blessings of grace into our lives. The future isn't over. It is only beginning. Regardless of what life has been until now, a better future can be shaped.

INFLUENCE

We now come to God's heart to make Abraham a man (and nation) of influence.

> *I will bless you **and make your name great*** (Genesis 12:2).

As the Lord continued to speak to me from this passage, I came to the phrase, "and make your name great." After some time meditating on this, I realized that God was speaking of influence. Our influence in our families, in our communities, and in the church is programmed to increase as we walk in the purpose that God has for us.

Those with great influence are those who have grown strong in the grace that God has given them. Great musicians have spent years working with their gift of music. Great athletes have spent countless hours training. Great men and women of God have spent their lives pursuing and developing the gifts that God has placed in them. From the willingness to separate, "see," and discover, we find that the blessing of God and, as a result, our influence in the lives of others grows.

Though the purpose of God for my life has unfolded slowly over many years, my faithfulness to God's grace and purpose has opened doors of tremendous influence. In just the past decade, after walking with God some 40 years, the opportunities for influence have exploded. This book is an example of something that I never actively pursued or knew how to pursue, but the opportunity was offered in this season of my life. No one was asking me to write a book 20 years ago. But because of my dedication to the teaching purpose that God put in my heart, the time of influence has arrived. It is not that I haven't had influence on different levels along the way. There have been many lives touched during our years of serving Him. But the last few years have opened the doors to an opportunity to touch thousands around the world on a daily basis.

God desires that we all be "salt and light" in this world. He desires that we have influence for good in the lives of others. If we return to the subject of the seed, we can see that some harvests take time.

I remember a speaker once holding up a small, green apple and asking the audience what was wrong with the apple. People began to call out that the apple was small, bitter, and not ripe. It was useless. It is interesting how we respond to the way a question is worded. The question encouraged the listeners to observe what was wrong, not what was right about the apple. As the speaker continued, it was pointed out that the apple was actually perfect. It was the perfect size and at the perfect stage of development for its future. It wasn't ready to be harvested. It wasn't ready to be made into a pie. For where it was at this moment, all was well. It was the size and color it was supposed to be. Its influence remained in the future and was yet to be realized.

Many times we become disgruntled with the present and don't realize that we may be exactly where we are supposed to be. We are in the process of growth and discovery. If we continue to keep our hearts separated unto Him, walking in the light of what we can see and growing in the gifts God has given, the blessing and influence will be there. Everything in God's Kingdom that has His life will grow, prosper, and multiply. That is the nature of God. Increase and influence will always follow a life that is separated unto Him.

BEING A BLESSING

Now we come to the actual purpose that God had in mind for Abraham from the beginning. Remember that we have seen the idea of separation which brings a clarity of vision, which allows us to discover our gifts and grow in them, which in turn releases the blessing and provision that we need in every season of life, which then opens the doors of influence in the world in which we live. These are important truths that can propel you into a future that perhaps you never imagined. But what was God's motivation behind this journey?

> *Now the Lord had said to Abram: "**Get out** of your country, from your family and from your father's house, to a land that **I will show you. I will make you** a great nation; **I will bless you** and **make your name great; and you shall be a blessing**" (Genesis 12:1-2).*

We have looked at these two verses phrase by phrase in order to understand how to cooperate with and shape the future that God has in mind for us. The last phrase sums up God's intention for all of us. *"And you shall be a blessing!"* At the end of the day, that is God's heart and should always be our heart. God is the greatest "blesser" there is. It is only normal that He would want His children to reflect His heart for the world. *Your future will always include blessing others.* Whether you are a mom with small children, a business person, a teacher, civil servant, musician, or minister, God's grace and purpose for your life is to bless others.

No matter where you are today in the journey of life, you can begin to shape your future. *You may have lost time, but you will never lose God's purpose and grace.* Are you willing to separate your heart unto Him and step into the future? It was given to you in Christ before time began!

CHAPTER 13

SHAPING
THE FUTURE
WITH MONEY

I UNDERSTAND that the subject of money is sensitive and often abused. However, I believe that if we can understand God's heart in the area of true prosperity, we will be able to grasp the power of money to shape our futures.

First, let's discuss prosperity. It is a hot button topic for many. What is prosperity? When we fully understand true prosperity, money will take its place in our hearts as a tool and not as a "god."

When we were born again, we moved from death to life and darkness to light in our spirits. We became a new creation, born again in righteousness.

But God, who is rich in mercy, because of His great love with which He loved us, even when we were dead in trespasses, made us alive together with

Christ (by grace you have been saved) (Ephesians 2:4-5).

Therefore, if anyone is in Christ, he is a new creation; old things have passed away; behold, all things have become new (2 Corinthians 5:17).

If spiritual death (separation from God) can be understood as poverty, then spiritual life is prosperity. The fact that we have eternal life and a future with God that is everlasting is the ultimate prosperity.

As we learn to live from our re-born spirits, the fruit of the Spirit becomes evident in our souls. Love, joy, peace, patience, etc. become our new normal for how we relate to the world around us. We could call this prosperity of the soul.

But the fruit of the Spirit is love, joy, peace, longsuffering, kindness, goodness, faithfulness, gentleness, self-control (Galatians 5:22-23).

The poverty of bitterness, hate, fear, and depression has been replaced with God's own nature. The joy of the Lord becomes our strength.

The renewing of our minds to truth can be considered mental prosperity. The more we grow in wisdom and the knowledge of God, the poverty of ignorance is replaced with the prosperity of the mind of Christ. We can think God's thoughts.

And do not be conformed to this world, but be transformed by the renewing of your mind, that

*you may prove what is that good and acceptable
and perfect will of God* (Romans 12:2).

Health and healing are physical prosperity. Learning to
appropriate God's promises for our bodies halts the poverty
of sickness and broken health.

*Beloved, I pray that you may prosper in all things
and be in health, just as your soul prospers* (3 John
1:2).

Walking in love toward those in our lives can be called
relational prosperity. As believers we should be experiencing
ever-increasing, positive relationships and blessed families.
A life filled with broken relationships and heartaches is a life
of relational poverty. Prosperity in relationships is God's will.

*Beloved, let us love one another, for love is of God;
and everyone who loves is born of God and knows
God* (1 John 4:7).

From the foundation of spiritual, emotional, mental,
physical, and relational prosperity, we can now understand
money and resources from a healthier point of view. Money
is simply an extension of what is in our hearts. A prosperous heart will have no fear of the subject of money. A poverty-stricken heart will flinch and become offended. Prosperity
must exist in the heart and impact the whole man before
money can be understood in its proper context.

What is money? Money is a measure of time in the form
of currency. Time encompasses the past, present, and future.
Money is usually tied to the past. If you work 40 hours a

week and are compensated with money, then the money is the value of the time that was spent to earn it. It is the value of the past.

What you do with money impacts the present, and as we will see, it can impact the future as well. What you do with money is a reflection of the prosperity of your heart. A selfish, poverty-stricken heart will use money to indulge the flesh and only grudgingly consider others. Bills may not get paid and care for the family may not be the first priority. The same money that can buy drugs or alcohol can be used to buy school supplies for a child. Once again, the visionary determines the possibilities.

When our eyes are only focused on the present, money is limited in its potential. Money is the past in the form of currency, but it exists in the present to do good or evil in the present or the future. How we treat ourselves and others with money reveals what we truly value.

HOW TO
SHAPE THE FUTURE WITH MONEY

Can money shape the future? Absolutely! In fact, your money is shaping your future, either actively or passively, whether you know it or not. It is when we understand money as seed that the possibilities of God are unleashed. Paul addressed the potential of the free will offering in 2 Corinthians 9.

> *Therefore I thought it necessary to exhort the brethren to go to you ahead of time, and prepare*

*your generous gift beforehand, which you had pre-
viously promised, that it may be ready as a matter of generosity and not as a grudging obligation.
But this I say: He who sows sparingly will also reap
sparingly, and he who sows bountifully will also
reap bountifully* (2 Corinthians 9:5-6).

Paul was speaking to the Corinthian believers about an
offering that was being collected to help others who were
suffering. If you read 2 Corinthians 8, you will see that the
subject of money was being discussed in detail. Chapter 9
continues the discussion.

Paul speaks of sowing and reaping within the realm of
money. A generous offering in Paul's mind is "sowing bountifully," and an offering given begrudgingly is "sowing sparingly."
Paul makes it clear that money (the value of time already past)
can be given to shape the future. "He who sows bountifully
will also reap (future) bountifully." This is an incredible truth
that can have everything to do with our futures.

Sowing is giving something you have in order to bring
blessing to others, to worship God, and to participate in the
expansion of the Kingdom. Sowing, reaping, giving, and
receiving are the clearest teachings in the Bible. Not only
is sowing and reaping a natural law, it is a spiritual law. As
we have discussed earlier, the spiritual law is what makes
the natural law possible. "What is seen was not made out of
things that are visible" (see Heb. 11:3). The invisible world of
the Spirit is the foundation for the visible world in which we
live. If sowing and reaping exists on earth, it is because it is a
reflection of a heavenly truth.

Sowing money into the Kingdom is a part of God's plan of increase. Let me hasten to mention that economic increase should not be divorced from the principles of work, integrity, patience, love, and wisdom. Remember, the subject of money should never be approached apart from the prosperity we have discussed earlier. If your heart is not prosperous, the subject of money can quickly become unbalanced. Nevertheless, giving is the very nature of God. God is Love and Love gives. God had a Son, but He wanted a family. He gave His Son in order to reap you and me. Jesus is the seed of the promise that God made to Abraham to bless all the families of the earth. Just as Jesus was sown into the earth in order to harvest a family, money or resources of any kind can become seed and impact our futures.

As I mentioned earlier, Elijah demanded food and water of the widow woman. Her offering was the seed that opened the door to her and her son's survival for over three years. Jesus received the offering of bread and fish and multiplied it to feed 5,000 men. Jesus said to give, and it would be given unto us pressed down, shaken together, and running over. God saw the giving and heard the prayers of Cornelius and sent an angel to change his destiny (see Acts 10). Paul encouraged cheerful giving and explained how such giving would unleash "all grace" in order that the givers would have an abundance for every good deed (see 2 Cor. 9:6-11). In each case, money and resources were changing the future.

Giving is not a get rich quick scheme. It is not a formula for easy wealth. It is simply one aspect of a transformed life that has grasped how the Kingdom was designed to operate.

"But seek first the kingdom of God and His righteousness, and all these things shall be added to you" (Matt. 6:33). Increase is the nature of the Kingdom. It is the nature of the gospel. It is grace in action!

"Whatever a man sows, that he will also reap" (Gal. 6:7). This principle exists in every area of life and cannot be turned off in the realm of money. Money is a reflection of our lives. It is an extension of the treasure that is in our hearts. What we do with money establishes the value we place on the gospel.

> *Now you Philippians know also that in the beginning of the gospel, when I departed from Macedonia, no church shared with me **concerning giving and receiving** but you only* (Philippians 4:15).

Paul was not hesitant to mention both giving and receiving. The sacrificial sowing of the Philippians was followed with a promise of future harvest:

> *And my God shall supply all your need according to His riches in glory by Christ Jesus* (Philippians 4:19).

Your seed is a door to your destiny. Everything is seed. Your thoughts, words, actions, and resources can all be sown into the Kingdom and they will multiply according to their kind.

Giving is the fruit of righteousness.

> *The righteous gives and does not spare* (Proverbs 21:26).

In every fruit there is a seed. In every seed there is a harvest. In every harvest there is provision. There is bread to eat and seed to sow. God's grace is in the seed. The writer of Proverbs understood the fruit of righteousness. Right standing with God, free from guilt, fear, and stress, transforms us from those who hoard into those who give.

Satan steals. Fear hoards. God gives. Be like God. Give love, give forgiveness, give time, give words of encouragement, give gifts. Give abundant life a chance.

> *Satan steals.*
> *Fear hoards.*
> *God gives.*

Sadly, in some circles the truth of sowing and reaping is under attack. When the topic of sowing, reaping, and giving and receiving comes up, the religious and fearful suddenly begin to sound like unbelievers.

They will acknowledge sowing and reaping in nature, in biology, in behavior, and in words, but when the topic turns to money they quickly get uncomfortable. They believe it is unseemly to talk about money in the context of the gospel message.

Those who criticize sowing and reaping aren't against money itself. They aren't against most offerings. They aren't against giving. They may even proudly proclaim that they are generous givers. What they struggle with is the expectation that God would somehow multiply one's giving. They think it is wrong to expect increase from God as a result of giving. They are especially against ministers of the Gospel going near the subject. In reality, though they may preach grace, they are taking a stand against grace in the realm of material increase.

Some cringe at the idea of a God who rewards generosity. They believe it is greed to expect a harvest for financial sowing. They redefine contentment to mean resignation and encourage struggling believers to find peace in their poverty. Meanwhile, the untapped abundance of grace lies dormant like a package of seeds in a cupboard.

Grace is about increase. If you are walking in grace, you are walking in increase. Grace flows from the principle of the seed. Future provision and abundance are found in the seeds of our thoughts, words, actions, attitudes, and resources. Increase is designed into every seed. Be intentional in your sowing. Whatsoever a man sows, that he will also reap! The harvest is always larger than the seed that conceived it.

AN OBLIGATION OR A SEED?

The difference between the giving that multiplies all grace to you and the giving that simply empties your checking account is faith. Many give dutifully but without faith. Their giving is an obligation with no hope attached. Others give in faith with a vision for the future and an expectation of God's blessing. Their giving is a seed. A dollar can be simply a dollar, or by faith and vision it can become a seed that will bless someone and multiply in some way. It is the heart of the giver that determines the potential of the dollar.

When our giving is wrapped in faith and love, it is empowered to bring in a harvest. When it is an obligation devoid of faith, it is simply an offering that will bless the recipient but carries no power for multiplication. This is why many Christians get offended with giving. They have given and given, fully aware of the promises of God over such giving, but their giving isn't a seed. It is an obligation not birthed in faith. Notice the difference between the offering of Cain and the offering of Abel.

> **By faith** Abel offered to God a more excellent sacrifice than Cain, through which he obtained witness that he was righteous, God testifying of his gifts (Hebrews 11:4).

Consider carefully what is being said in the above verse. God testified (and still does) of Abel's *gift*. In fact, by his gift he obtained the witness that he was righteous! What was the difference between Abel's gift and Cain's gift? What caused God to "testify of his gifts"? *By faith,* Abel offered to God a more excellent sacrifice. It wasn't the kind of offering he gave, but the condition of the heart. Abel's heart of faith activated his offering to be considered "more excellent." It was a sacrifice wrapped in faith.

Both were sacrificing, but Cain's offering was a sacrifice without faith. Abel's offering moved him into another dimension. By faith his sacrifice became a seed of righteousness. It is our faith in the goodness of God that turns a sacrifice into a seed, and a seed carries many harvests within.

That is why Paul declared that God loves a "cheerful giver."

> God loves a cheerful giver. And God is able to make all grace abound toward you, that you, always

having all sufficiency in all things, may have an abundance for every good work (2 Corinthians 9:7-8).

A cheerful giver is a faith filled giver. A cheerful giver unlocks the grace of multiplication in all things. *A cheerful giver is changing the future with money!*

Money won't make you happy, but neither will poverty. The purpose of money is to meet needs and bless others. If our money is the extension of a prosperous heart, it will carry the faith to bring increase. Money can shape the future.

We have no problem with this concept in the world of education. Students pay tens of thousands of dollars to get a degree that will hopefully enhance their future. Money is spent to buy products that we believe will make life more enjoyable. Money buys vacations. Money is simply a tool of exchange.

> *A cheerful giver is changing the future with money!*

But money invested in the things of God has greater potential than most of us realize. If we give in faith (the expectation of God's goodness), we are touching both the natural world and the spiritual world. It is in the world of the Spirit that multiplication takes place and the blessings of God overtake us.

There is grace for money and potential grace *in* money. Money can be a seed that carries great potential, or it can be a tool for lust and greed. Once again, *it is the visionary who*

determines the destiny of the seed. How is money shaping your
future? Your money will bear the nature of its source—you.

CHAPTER 14

SHAPING THE FUTURE WITH YOUR ATTITUDE

S O much of our present and our future is a reflection of our attitude and outlook on life. Two people facing the same set of circumstances can have two entirely different attitudes and experience two entirely different results. Paul spoke of this while in prison as he wrote the Philippians:

According to my earnest expectation and hope that in nothing I shall be ashamed (Philippians 1:20).

In this verse, Paul speaks of earnest expectation and hope. Paul had a positive outlook and an attitude of expectation.

Paul's words reveal a fundamental outlook that shaped his future. In spite of the persecution that he endured for the sake of the gospel, Paul's approach to life was positive. Although he knew that his call would involve hardship and ultimately death, he was able to live his life with expectation and hope. Listen to the final words we have of Paul in his last letter to Timothy:

> For I am already being poured out as a drink offering, and the time of my departure is at hand. I have fought the good fight, **I have finished the race,** I have kept the faith. Finally, **there is laid up for me the crown of righteousness,** which the Lord, the righteous Judge, will give to me on that Day, and not to me only but also to all who have loved His appearing (2 Timothy 4:6-8).

In spite of the incredible hardships that were a part of Paul's "race," he was able to finish while keeping faith. And Paul was still anticipating the future beyond death. The "crown of righteousness" was his goal. Consider these closing words in 2 Timothy:

> Also I was delivered out of the mouth of the lion. **And the Lord will deliver me from every evil work and preserve me for His heavenly kingdom** (2 Timothy 4:17-18).

Again, we find a positive attitude that was shaping Paul's future. His earnest expectation and hope were being fulfilled.

Much about our futures is determined by our attitudes. In our modern way of speaking, we are either optimists or pessimists. We all have a general approach to life that sets the tone for how we respond to and evaluate our circumstances and possibilities.

Let's consider a very powerful example, again from the life of Paul. Paul and his traveling companion, Silas, had been imprisoned for preaching the gospel. They had been beaten with rods and thrown into an "inner prison" and their feet were fastened in stocks. Most of us would find an opportunity to complain. Silas could have blamed Paul for their circumstances. They could have been fighting among themselves as they contemplated years in prison or, worse, execution. Attitude is a powerful force. Our expectation in the goodness of God can overcome the evil of men. Let's see what happened.

> *But at midnight Paul and Silas were praying and singing hymns to God, and the prisoners were listening to them. Suddenly there was a great earthquake, so that the foundations of the prison were shaken; and immediately all the doors were opened and everyone's chains were loosed* (Acts 16:25-26).

We will respond to the events of life according to the attitude and expectation we carry within. That attitude will then determine the future possibilities. Rather than arguing and complaining about a seemingly impossible situation, Paul and Silas chose to pray and praise God. *Complaining never unleashes the power of God, but praise will.* Praise is an act of glorifying God regardless of the circumstances, but it also unleashes the power of God to change the circumstances! One way or another, the heart that lives to give thanks and believe will see the goodness of God. David understood praise to be the gateway to increase and blessing!

> *Let the peoples praise You, O God; let all the peoples praise You.* **Then the earth shall yield her increase; God, our own God, shall bless us** (Psalm 67:5-6).

It is interesting that the potential of "increase" in the earth and blessing in our lives is dependent upon our recognition of God's goodness!

> *Complaining never unleashes the power of God, but praise will.*

God's delivering power is released through the praises of those who trust Him. The attitude of thanksgiving, expectancy, and hope is a major force in shaping our futures. The moment our expectancy is diminished and our hearts begin to "see" a negative outcome, we lose the power to bring change. Our futures are in our hearts. *God's blessings and increase are released in the lives of the thankful.* A thankful heart is one that is flowing in the grace of God and is not shaped by the corruption that is in the world.

I have known many over the years whose hearts are negative toward just about everything. I must say that I have been one of those people at times. It is an approach to life that may recognize God's goodness on a theological level, but on a practical level life is lived from our own strength, our own logic, and our own resources. Of course, our strength, logic, and resources will never be enough, and the negative attitude begins to grow.

Once the heart grows hard toward the present and the future, words of negativity will begin to flow. This attitude can be seen and heard through body language, complaining, criticism, gossip, and how we react to every piece of potentially negative news.

Rather than a default setting of praise and thanksgiving in our hearts, there is a fundamental approach to life as a victim. Unknowingly, we are shutting off God's provision by ignoring His vision for our lives. We have chosen to see the issues around us as more powerful than the God who lives in us. Rather than praising God for His goodness, we begin to exalt the circumstances through complaining and fear. Rather than receiving His grace and provision by faith, we begin to contemplate hardship and loss.

In both scenarios, the future is being shaped. The praises of Paul and Silas in prison set them free both literally and figuratively. *You won't be bound by something you don't allow to control you.* Your future must be settled in your heart and the vision of God's purpose for your life must be more powerful than the challenges around you. The expectation of good, of blessings, of health, loving relationships, and future influence in the world must begin within. As we have seen, prosperity begins within. Vision begins within. We shape our futures in our hearts.

You can tell who will have a joyful future and who won't by their attitude toward the present. So often we see the complainers setting the course of their lives by how they approach the challenges of today. For the pessimist, the expectation of difficulties, hardships, relationship problems, and financial problems is allowed to suffocate any hint of God's overwhelming goodness. Praise is the last thing in their heart. In five years, it will be the same. If there is no heart change, there will be no positive future.

The future God carries in His heart for us will be limited to the possibilities that we see with our hearts. God's heart toward His children is filled with possibilities. Our future in God's mind is filled with grace, potential, and increase.

> *For I know the thoughts that I think toward you, says the Lord, thoughts of peace and not of evil, to give you a future and a hope* (Jeremiah 29:11).

In spite of the corruption in the world, God has made provision for us to have His peace, His love, His joy, His faith, and shape our futures with the seeds of life, His promises. Your attitude is a powerful force for or against the future that God desires for you.

CHAPTER 15

SHAPING THE FUTURE BY FAITH

W HAT if your future took its shape from your faith? What kind of a future would you be looking at? We know that faith is the evidence of things not seen and the substance of things hoped for. Faith is about the future.

> *Now faith is the substance of things hoped for, the evidence of things not seen* (Hebrews 11:1).

We are all projecting something into our futures. We can be projecting our pasts into our futures, or our fears, or our limited resources, or our current health challenges. Or we can be projecting the vision of ever-increasing blessings, peace, joy, and love. Something is being projected. The future is being shaped by the vision of your heart.

When we read the great faith chapter, Hebrews 11, we can begin to see how the faith of those mentioned shaped their futures. The willingness to step out of the current circumstances and into the promise of God unleashed the purpose and grace that God had intended for their lives. Let's look at some examples.

> **By faith** Noah, being divinely warned of things not yet seen, moved with godly fear, **prepared an ark** (Hebrews 11:7).

Noah was activated by a word from God. Noah's future and that of his family was shaped by faith in God's Word. He had never seen rain and probably had no idea what was in store for the earth, but his future followed his faith. He prepared an ark.

> **By faith** Abraham obeyed when he was called to go out to the place which he would receive as an inheritance. And he went out, **not knowing where he was going** (Hebrews 11:8).

The call of God on Abraham's life did not include a clear picture what was in store for him. But his obedience (faith in action), unleashed God's grace for his life, his family, and the purpose of God that transcended Abraham's own understanding.

> **By faith** Sarah herself also **received strength** to conceive seed, and she bore a child when she was past the age, **because she judged Him faithful** who had promised (Hebrews 11:11).

Though Sarah's first reaction to the promise of God was to laugh (see Gen. 18:12), she later believed the promise and her body conformed to her faith! Many would be healed today if they would understand this great truth. *We don't receive our healing when our body tells us we have it. We receive our healing when we choose to receive it by faith. Let your body conform to the reality of your faith!* The moment that Sarah judged God faithful, her future changed. Have you judged Him faithful? Your future depends on it.

> **By faith** Abraham, when he was tested, offered up Isaac, and he who had received the promises offered up his only begotten son, of whom it was said, "In Isaac your seed shall be called," **concluding that God was able to raise him up, even from the dead** (Hebrews 11:17-19).

Abraham's future and the future of God's promise to him rested on an action that to the natural mind made no sense. But faith shaped the future. Faith concluded that God was able to raise Isaac even from the dead to accomplish His promise.

How many of us are facing situations that seem to be dead? Are we willing to let the "dead" circumstances be the future, or can we with the eyes of faith see God's resurrection power bringing life and renewed purpose to those circumstances? As we have discussed, what we see in our hearts is the picture we carry of our futures. We must let God's promises paint His picture in our hearts and allow faith to breathe life into the possibilities.

> **By faith** Isaac blessed Jacob and Esau **concerning things to come** (Hebrews 11:20).

Isaac trusted God for the future of his sons and blessed them with that confidence in his heart. Faith looks ahead. Faith birthed from God's promises will speak those promises over the future. Faith will bless the future of our marriages, our children, our jobs, and our health. The faith that activates from hearing God is the most powerful force we have to shape our futures. In the same way, fear and unbelief shape the futures of many. Independence from God does not carry the promise of abundant life.

My future with Andrew Wommack Ministries and Charis Bible College was shaped by a word from God and a step of faith. While on a trip to Colorado to see Andrew's ministry and Charis Bible College, I heard the Lord speak to me clearly that "one day I would teach there." I could have easily talked myself out of believing His word to me. No one in Colorado knew me. I could have decided that it was too complicated to move from Dallas to Colorado Springs with no certain job. I could have hesitated and allowed worldly concerns shape my future. But I believed God, and today I am living in the future that was conceived by faith from a word from God.

Faith shapes the future!

> *By faith Jacob, when he was dying, **blessed** each of the sons of Joseph, and worshiped, leaning on the top of his staff. **By faith** Joseph, when he was dying, made mention of the departure of the children of Israel, and **gave instructions** concerning his bones* (Hebrews 11:21-22).

As we move through Hebrews 11, we continue to find those who were of faith looking toward the future. Their words of blessing, prophecy, and instructions carried the power of God that had been stirred in their hearts. Rather than doubting, questioning, and complaining, these faith giants determined to cooperate with the One who had a purpose for the future. It may only take one faith filled person to change the destiny of many.

By faith, Moses's parents were not afraid of the king's command (see Heb. 11:23).

By faith Moses refused the pleasures of sin because he had his eyes on the reward of the future (see Heb. 11:24-26).

> **By faith** *he forsook Egypt, not fearing the wrath of the king;* **for he endured as seeing Him who is invisible** (Hebrews 11:27).

Moses chose the future over the present. Moses chose to see Him who is invisible over the very visible threats of the king of Egypt. Moses shaped his future by faith.

Faith is the spiritual force that God has given us to unlock the blessings of the future. Faith sees, speaks, and acts based upon an invisible potential that has been made real in the heart of the believer. Faith flows from dependence on the voice of God.

> *So then faith comes by hearing, and hearing by the word of God* (Romans 10:17).

The more we are connected to the Source, the more we are equipped to shape our futures. The future isn't set in stone. Though we can see through prophetic scriptures how the world will continue to crumble before the return of Jesus,

> *The more we are connected to the Source, the more we are equipped to shape our futures.*

our own lives and futures don't have to crumble. Jesus was very aware of the corruption of this world when He gave us His incredible promises of abundant life. Jesus and the New Testament authors gave us wonderful promises by the Holy Spirit, in the midst of Roman persecution, and prophecies concerning tribulation in the future. *The possibility of a blessed future is still a promise in a fallen world!*

When we get right down to it, the futures of the world and of governments, culture, marriages, children, careers, and ministries are all being shaped by either fear or faith. And humans are doing the shaping. God is not orchestrating the details of your future. He has provided grace for you to shape your future in the midst of a fallen world.

The woman with the issue of blood could have resigned herself to a future of physical suffering and an early death. But upon hearing of Jesus and His goodness, a vision of a better future was conceived in her heart. Her vision moved her to touch the hem of Jesus's garment. Jesus responded by declaring that her faith had changed her present and certainly her future.

> *And He said to her, "Daughter, **your faith has made you well**. Go in peace, and be healed of your affliction"* (Mark 5:34).

In an instant, her life was changed. Do you see it? She could have stayed home and complained. She could have felt bitter that Jesus had not come to her house. But a vision in her heart (your future springs from your heart) inspired her to walk in faith to find Jesus, and the rest of her life was changed.

The blind beggar Bartimaeus had a similar experience. His life had been spent in blindness and begging. But when he heard that Jesus was passing by, a vision was born in his heart. His future hung in the balance. He could remain polite and quiet, or he could call out to Jesus. Jesus heard the cry of faith and stopped for Bartimaeus. That encounter changed his life forever.

> *Then Jesus said to him, "Go your way; **your faith has made you well.**" And immediately he received his sight and followed Jesus on the road* (Mark 10:52).

A passive Bartimaeus would have died a blind beggar. But a vision in his heart changed his life. Faith was activated and his future was transformed.

In both of these examples and in many more that could be listed, it was the faith of simple people that changed their futures. Jesus could have said, "Your faith has changed your future, go in peace."

Will your future be shaped by fear or faith? You are equipped by God to hear Him, believe Him, and act upon His Word. You are purposed for a positive future. Will you cooperate?

SHAPING
THE FUTURE
THROUGH PRAYER

WHILE this is not a book about prayer, I would be remiss to not include a chapter that looks at prayer in the light of shaping the future. Prayer is always about the future! Whether the answer comes in seconds, days, months, or years, the future is being touched.

For some, prayer may be one of the more mysterious, misunderstood, or neglected areas of their lives. When we aren't quite sure why we are praying, or if we don't understand the potential that exists, prayer can become a lifeless duty. For some it is a religious obligation. For others it is simply mental hope that maybe God will get involved in whatever situation is of concern.

We must remember that God gave the earth to man (see Ps. 115:16), and His involvement in the affairs of men is activated through our believing prayer. Beyond the richness of simply fellowshipping with the Father, prayer is the spiritual potential God has given us to literally change the future! If we could get a revelation of the incredible power that we have as believers, prayer would no longer be a mystery and duty but an opportunity to shape lives, circumstances, and destinies.

Jesus ministered from what He received from the Father:

> *Most assuredly, I say to you, the Son can do nothing of Himself, but what He sees the Father do; for whatever He does, the Son also does in like manner* (John 5:19).

The secret to the future is in the fellowship we have today with the Father. Jesus was limited to what He saw. He wasn't making up ministry as He went. What He saw in fellowship (prayer) with the Father became the future for those who sought Him. Healing, deliverance, forgiveness, and provision were all in the future when Jesus "saw" what the Father was doing. Jesus then ministered from that vision or revelation. That is the power of prayer. Jesus's prayer life impacted the futures of people in need.

> *The secret to the future is in the fellowship we have today with the Father.*

If we would approach prayer with that in mind, it would become an exciting way to change destinies, including our own.

Praying for people's hearts, relationships, marriages, children, physical needs, resources, and wisdom are all adventures into the future. If we can see the Father's heart for these situations and people, we could become the channel through which their lives and circumstances are changed. In that light, prayer is the opportunity that God has given us to shape the future.

Prayer is not a religious duty, but rather a fellowship with the Father that can be as normal as speaking to a friend or a spouse. I find myself talking with God throughout the day, sharing my heart and being sensitive to His voice in my spirit. There are times when I make declarations of His promises, times when I give thanks, times when I believe I receive from Him, and times when I lift up others. Prayer releases the grace of God into the lives and circumstances of mankind.

Prayer releases the grace of God into the lives and circumstances of mankind.

God's means of changing lives are in our hands. It is our prayer, our loving, our forgiving, our words, our actions, our giving, and our serving that release God's grace as a seed into the hearts of others. *Everything we sow in prayer into the world of the Spirit is a seed that carries the heart of God for someone's future.*

Are your prayers really important? Consider the following instruction that Jesus gave to His disciples:

Therefore pray the Lord of the harvest to send out laborers into His harvest (Matthew 9:38).

I always found it curious that Jesus would ask the disciples to pray that God would do that which He obviously wanted to do anyway. Can't God just decide to raise up laborers for the harvest? Isn't that foremost in His heart? And yet, Jesus commanded that we pray for such a thing. *Could it be that God's will does not automatically happen apart from the cooperation of His children?* What if we don't pray for laborers? The future of nations depends upon God sending out laborers into the world, but the future of the laborers depends upon the prayers of believers! This may be startling to some, but I can find no other explanation for Jesus's words.

Let's look at some more examples. Consider Paul's experience in the book of Acts:

> *Now it happened, when I returned to Jerusalem and was praying in the temple, that I was in a trance and saw Him saying to me, "Make haste and get out of Jerusalem quickly, for they will not receive your testimony concerning Me"* (Acts 22:17-18).

Paul went to the Temple to pray. He could have easily decided to go to the gym to work out or go to a coffee shop for coffee. There is nothing wrong with either of those activities, but it was in prayer that Paul "saw" and "heard" the Lord. The warning to leave Jerusalem was urgent and very much tied to Paul's future. Prayer not only shapes the futures of others but can be critical in us receiving instructions from the Lord for our own futures.

Paul encouraged others to pray for his ministry. Why?

Finally, brethren, pray for us, that the word of the Lord may run swiftly and be glorified, just as it is with you (2 Thessalonians 3:1).

Some would think that if God called Paul to travel and preach, God would automatically ensure that the word of the Lord would be glorified. But if that was so, why did Paul ask for prayer for that very thing? I believe Paul realized the power of believing prayer based upon the vision that was in his heart and hopefully in the hearts of those who joined him in prayer. Prayer shapes the future.

John prayed for believers in the opening verses of his third epistle:

Beloved, I pray that you may prosper in all things and be in health, just as your soul prospers (3 John 2).

Here we find John praying for prosperity and emotional and physical health for his readers. We know that Jesus went to the cross and rose from the dead to give us abundant life. We have many, many scriptures and promises that declare God's heart for these things. Nevertheless, John was praying for something that was already God's will for His children. It is through prayer that God's heart flows through our hearts and into the "natural" dimension of human need. Believers are to be the channels through which the grace of God is sown into lives and circumstances. Just because something is God's will doesn't mean it will happen apart from the faith of His children.

When we realize that prayer is the means through which His will comes to pass, we will become much more active in seeing ourselves as divine agents of change. Your life and the lives of those around you need divine influence. They need the seeds of love, forgiveness, and peace. Prayer sows those seeds. Prayer sees God's heart for others and allows His heart to become our heart. From there we speak words of blessing, healing, and provision.

We cannot make someone do something against their will through prayer, but we can bring the influence of the Holy Spirit into their circumstances. Jesus prayed for us before His arrest and crucifixion! While praying for His disciples in John 17, he looked into the future and saw you and me.

> *I do not pray for these alone, **but also for those who will believe** in Me through their word* (John 17:20).

In this chapter, Jesus was praying His final prayer to the Father before being arrested and led away to His trial and crucifixion. His prayer is revealing in many ways as He reports to the Father at the end of His mission on earth. In the prayer Jesus begins by focusing specifically on His disciples, but then shifts to "those who will believe in Me through their word." This is an obvious choice in the heart of Jesus to envision the future and to see you and me. His Word has spread around the globe in the last 2,000 years, and millions have believed. Jesus was praying for them and us. In fact, He still does.

> *Therefore He is also able to save to the uttermost those who come to God through Him, since*

He always lives to make intercession for them
(Hebrews 7:25).

This is another indicator that God's desire and will do not automatically happen. If Jesus continues to pray for us, then prayer must be important. And prayer is always about the future.

One effective way to pray is to pray as Paul prayed for the believers. Several times in his epistles to the church, Paul stopped to pray and he recorded his prayer. These prayers are extremely helpful for us to see not only Paul's heart, but God's heart for us. I have no doubt that Paul was expressing what he saw in his time with the Father.

> [I] *do not cease to give thanks for you, making mention of you in my prayers: that the God of our Lord Jesus Christ, the Father of glory, may give to you the spirit of wisdom and revelation in the knowledge of Him, the eyes of your understanding being enlightened; that you may know what is the hope of His calling, what are the riches of the glory of His inheritance in the saints, and what is the exceeding greatness of His power toward us who believe* (Ephesians 1:16-20).

Paul prays that the believers would have a "spirit of wisdom and revelation in the knowledge of Him." This spirit of wisdom and revelation is therefore not automatic. It is to be received through growing in the knowledge of Him. Paul is praying that the believers would continue to seek the Lord and grow in wisdom and revelation. This has everything to do with how the future of these believers will unfold. *"My people are destroyed for lack of knowledge"* (Hos. 4:6). Ignorance of God, His nature, and His purposes has been the reason so many believers live frustrated lives. Paul is praying for people like us to grow in the knowledge of Him.

"The eyes of your understanding being enlightened." The eyes of our understanding refer to a spiritual enlightenment. Revelation knowledge describes our spiritual understanding being made alive to the things of God and the potential that we as believers have to shape the future. Jesus rebuked the people of Israel for their spiritual blindness.

> *For the hearts of this people have grown dull. Their ears are hard of hearing, and their eyes they have closed, **lest they should see with their eyes** and hear with their ears, lest they should understand with their hearts and turn, so that I should heal them* (Matthew 13:15).

Jesus was pointing out the desperate need of the people in His time. I don't believe it is any different today. Hearts are dull, spiritual hearing is minimal, and spiritual vision is limited. These are the keys to shaping the future, and prayer is the key to opening our hearts to God's possibilities. Jesus gave us an incredible prayer promise:

> *Therefore I say to you, whatever things you ask when you pray, believe that you receive them, and you will have them* (Mark 11:24).

In one of Jesus's most well-known statements concerning prayer, we again see the emphasis on shaping the future. We are expected to pray. We are expected to ask. The purpose and the blessings of God don't just happen. We are expected to believe we have the things God has shown us *before* we see them or experience them tangibly. And we are told that we "will have them." That is the future. *Our faith in the promises of God can bring into our lives the things that would not have happened or appeared without prayer.* How much have we missed of God's possibilities simply because we didn't bring it forth through prayer?

When we don't pray according to God's will for our future and the futures of others, we are actually limiting Him from moving in our lives. This may sound hard, but when we don't cooperate with God through prayer, we are allowing corruption and loss to continue in our lives and the lives of others.

Once we grasp the incredible potential we have for shaping the future, we will be far more motivated to spend time in the presence of God and "see" what He is doing. Our cooperation through prayer in the purposes of God will shape the future of our lives and the lives of those around us.

> *The effective, fervent prayer of a righteous man avails much* (James 5:16).

CHAPTER 17

WHAT IS YOUR IMAGE OF YOU?

ALL of us see ourselves a certain way. Our life experiences, our failures and successes, our education, our bank account, our physical appearance, our background, and the culture in which we were raised have created an image on the inside of us. That image, whether it is good or bad, true or false, is the dominant power that shapes our destiny. The image we carry inside can even block the blessings and purposes of God in our lives.

An image of unworthiness, guilt, and self-hatred will be projected into our relationships and circumstances. Those around us will respond to what we are projecting through our words, actions, body language, and attitude. Fear is a powerful image that can contaminate all of God's desired blessings in your life. The writer of Proverbs makes this brief statement, which carries such an incredible revelation:

For as he thinks in his heart, so is he (Proverbs 23:7).

The image we have over ourselves determines our attitude, expectancy, and faith. An image of sickness or lack will shape the future just as certainly as an image of justification by faith and peace with God. The heart is a powerful generator of the future!

As we have discussed throughout this book, the heart is where your future resides. Jesus made it very clear when He said:

A good man out of the good treasure of his heart brings forth good things, and an evil man out of the evil treasure brings forth evil things (Matthew 12:35).

We could expand this verse to speak of that which comes out of the heart of the joyful, the loving, and the generous versus that which comes from the heart of the bitter, the unforgiving, and the stingy.

The only difference between the life of abundance and the life of lack is the image that we have on the inside. How do you see yourself?

Are you a new creation, created in righteousness, adopted into the family of God, more than a conqueror, seated with Him, endued with power, worthy of every promise, and filled with His love? Or are you a poor sinner, focused on past failures, always concerned about not having enough, bitter at those who are blessed, filled with guilt or remorse, and always expecting the worst? What is your image of you?

As you think in your heart, you are determining your future. A negative future will come from a negative heart. An abundant future will come from a heart that has believed God's Word.

> *Keep your heart with all diligence, for out of it spring the issues of life* (Proverbs 4:23).

When you have God's vision for your life and purpose, whether it is for healing, for a ministry, a relationship, or for your career, it is a seed filled with potential. How you manage the vision will determine the scope of the harvest. If your image of you is negative, the vision of God that could have happened will be limited or stopped. The seeds in your heart will follow the vision of the visionary!

WHAT ABOUT A HEART THAT HAS SUFFERED REJECTION?

All of us have experienced rejection. Rejection is a powerful weapon against our self-worth. Rejection can breed thoughts of inadequacy, hopelessness, anger, bitterness, fear, and depression. Whether the rejection has been on the playground in school, from a romantic interest, from a potential employer, or from parents, rejection can cause great damage in how we see ourselves and our value to others. Rejection is a powerful force that can steal the future God has for you.

Rejection is the soil in which unbelief grows. Each time we experience a rejection, the potential for doubt and unbelief increases. How can you have faith in life, others, or yourself when you believe you are unlovely, incapable of being accepted, or inadequate in some way? *The seeds of rejection produce the harvest of failure.* Our identity becomes tied to the rejections we have experienced, and we set our expectations in life according to the memory of the rejections we carry in our hearts. This is nothing more than bondage and oppression.

> *Rejection is the soil in which unbelief grows. The seeds of rejection produce the harvest of failure.*

This same attitude we often carry into our relationship with God. If others don't like us, why would God? As a result, it is difficult if not impossible to enjoy a loving, trusting relationship with the Father. He sees all of our faults and is more aware of all of our weaknesses than anyone else! Why should we expect anything good from Him? We limit the future with such thoughts.

Listen to this: *"to the praise of the glory of His grace, by which He made us accepted in the Beloved"* (Eph. 1:6).

Did you understand what was said? In Ephesians 1, Paul declares that God has blessed us (v. 3), He has chosen us to be without blame before Him in love (v. 4), He has predetermined that we are sons and daughters in His family (not slaves or orphans) (v. 5), and by grace He has made us accepted (v. 6)! This is the nearly too good to be true Good News!

The Greek meaning of the word *accepted* is "to make graceful, charming, lovely, agreeable, to surround with favor and to honor with blessings." Wow!

Before you were ever conceived, God knew you and chose to love you and accept you. You may have been picked last on the playground, but you are first in the heart of God. You may not have Hollywood looks, but you couldn't look any better to God. You are unique. There is no one like you. You have divine potential and a divine purpose in this world. You have a future. You are accepted!

If you can get your heart wrapped around this, faith will spring forth. When we know that there is no chance of rejection from God, we can believe the promises, enjoy the fellowship, see our potential, and have peace. Your future can begin the moment your image of you reflects God's image of you.

Allow His image of you to take shape in your heart. Your future depends on it.

CHAPTER 18

THE SEEDS
OF YOUR FUTURE

A S we come to the end of this book, I am very aware that I have probably only scratched the surface of this incredible topic. Every day brings fresh understanding and new opportunities to shape the future.

One of the major truths that has set me free from so many religious concepts, fears, and uncertainties is the realization that *God is for me,* not against me. That simple truth has had a profound impact on the way I live life and approach the future. It dawned on me many years ago that God is not my problem. He is the answer for every problem and the giver of wisdom, peace, joy, love, and provision for every need. If God is for me, who can be against me? (See Romans 8:31.) Therefore, the future that God carries in His heart for me is good. While the fallen world, corrupt men, and the forces of darkness may interfere, I know that God has made His provision for victorious living available to me. I am not at the mercy of the corruption that is in the world. I have a role to play in my future and the futures of the ones I love.

Let's consider again a couple of well-known verses and dig a little deeper into God's heart and His provision for our lives.

> *For I know the thoughts that I think toward you, says the Lord, thoughts of peace and not of evil, **to give you a future** and a hope* (Jeremiah 29:11).

> *Now to Him who is able to do exceedingly abundantly above all that we ask or think, **according to the power that works in us*** (Ephesians 3:20).

In spite of the fallen world in which we live, and in spite of the obvious persecution and influence of evil men, God's heart toward His children is steadfast. His heart is for our increase and blessing. But it has everything to do with the power that is at work in us! We generate our futures through faith or fear, expectancy or dread, complaining or praise. We are the architects of our futures.

Jesus came that we might have abundant life, not just "barely getting by" life.

> *I have come that they may have life, and that they may have it more abundantly* (John 10:10).

As we have seen earlier, the future is contained in the seeds of the present. Therefore, the future, hope, and exceeding abundance of God's heart exists now *in seed form*. Where can we find it? Apart from all of the promises of God that have been discussed, there is another aspect of God's provision I want to consider with you. Paul declared that the Spirit that lives within us bears fruit.

> *But the fruit of the Spirit is love, joy, peace, longsuf-fering, kindness, goodness, faithfulness, gentleness, self-control* (Galatians 5:22-23).

Could this be a part of the "power that works in us"? Here we have a very clear reference to "fruit." As we saw in the Garden of Eden, the fruit of the Garden contained the seeds of God's provision for the future. Now, we have the Holy Spirit being discussed as having "fruit." The fruit is expressed as love, joy, peace, longsuffering, kindness, goodness, faith-fulness (faith), gentleness, and self-control. Think of these expressions of fruit as hanging from the Tree of Life in the Garden. What is in a fruit? A seed. It is a seed that carries within itself the heart of God for the future. It is a seed that is programmed to reproduce and multiply. It is the future.

If we accept that upon being born again, we have received the Spirit of God, and we are a new creation, then we need to understand that the nature of God (the fruit of the Spirit of God) lives in us *with the future in seed form.*

Do you want to shape your future? Begin to sow the nature of God (the seeds of the fruit of the Spirit) into those around you and into your circumstances. Rather than living on the surface level of emotional reactions, feelings, opinions, and selfishness, begin to see the seeds within you and sow them. You can sow love because the fruit within carries the seed of love for others. You can sow joy. You may think you missed out on joy, but you didn't. Perhaps you haven't chosen to "eat" that fruit, but if you are born again, it is in you. And it carries enough for you to share with others. You can sow peace. When others are losing control and full of fear and anxiety, you can be the giver of peace. You have it within. Longsuffering (patience), goodness, faithfulness, kindness, and self-control are all alive within you. They all have seeds for others if you choose to be a sower.

As we sow the seeds of God's nature (the fruit of the Spirit), we are shaping the future more than we can imagine. Loving others when perhaps they aren't deserving, or exhibiting self-control while others are out of control is sowing the seeds that may find receptive hearts. Perhaps those around you have never seen love or self-control before. Perhaps your decision to sow God's nature into a situation will be the seed that changes their lives.

When we choose to live from the Spirit, we are influencing the future. When we choose to move past our emotions and feelings, we are leaving the realm of darkness and confusion and bringing the light and life of God into the lives and situations we face. Consider this example of possible human reactions to a situation:

> *When we choose to live from the Spirit, we are influencing the future.*

A soft answer turns away wrath, but a harsh word stirs up anger (Proverbs 15:1).

We have probably all had moments when we spoke a harsh word, and we have probably all had moments of responding to a hard situation with a soft word. Each response shapes the future in a different way. A soft answer (self-control, gentleness, etc.) diffuses the wrath that could bring negative consequences. Harsh words (the flesh) create a different future. It is as simple as that.

God's heart for our futures is positive and abundant, but we are the visionaries and the deciders of what we will sow.

We can choose to be a blessing to our spouses no matter what. We can choose to shape our children with love and encouragement or with anger and impatience. Both kinds of seeds will produce a harvest.

We can choose to love the unlovely, forgive the undeserving, serve the immature, and bless those who despitefully use us (see Matt. 5:44). When we do, we are shaping not only our future, but the futures of others. Seeds carry the future and the nature of God is within us to shape the future.

The Lord made a powerful statement to Abraham many years ago that has become the foundation for how I live and what I expect in life.

> *Surely blessing I will bless you, and multiplying I will multiply you* (Hebrews 6:14).

God created all things, including Adam and Eve, with the future contained within in seeds of His creation. Nothing new has been added other than the Seed, Jesus. From the beginning, everything God had ever purposed for His creation was hidden in that which was visible. The invisible future will come from seeds.

Sin perverted God's purpose, but not His method. In order to "reverse the curse," God once again chose the seed principle. Jesus was of the lineage (seed) of Abraham and was conceived by the Word spoken to Mary. He became the "grain of wheat" that fell into the earth.

> *The hour has come that the Son of Man should be glorified. Most assuredly, I say to you, unless a grain of wheat falls into the ground and dies, it remains alone; but if it dies, it produces much grain* (John 12:23-24).

Jesus's redemptive work was fully realized by the principle of the seed. He was sown in order that we might be harvested.

Our entrance into Christ happened by receiving the incorruptible seed of His Word into our hearts and believing. As a new creation, we have the nature of God alive within us. That nature produces fruit. Within the fruit of God's nature there are seeds. The seeds of God's nature carry His heart and purpose for the future of individuals, families, and nations. We are "carriers" of the future!

What is God's heart for His "seeds" (His children)? I will say it again:

> *Surely blessing I will bless you, and multiplying I will multiply you* (Hebrews 6:14).

This is God's heart for you. This is God's purpose for your life. Though spoken directly to Abraham, it is now referring to us, the carriers of God's nature in seed form. Whatever you have come from or been through, however you see yourself, whatever have been your mistakes or failures, if you are born again, God's heart is to bless you and multiply you! Why?

Because you bear His nature in seed form. The fruit of the Spirit within carries your possible future and the possible futures of those whose lives you touch.

Seeds were meant to reproduce and multiply exceedingly abundantly more than we can ask or think (see Eph. 3:20). Your life is meant to experience increase, blessing, and multiplication.

When I saw this, I realized that I should only expect the best from God. The world may challenge me, but God is for me. Why? Because I carry His nature within, and the nature of God within me can shape the future of multitudes. It can change marriages, save children, heal the broken, and bind up the wounded. The nature of God within will attract the blessing of God without. You should expect to be blessed.

Sadly, many expect to be raked over the coals by God. They feel unworthy and undeserving. Religion and guilt have stolen their purpose. If you aren't walking in peace and joy, you've been robbed! You've been lied to. The fruit of God's nature lives in you, but religion and guilt may have slammed the door on that treasure. It is time to unleash the potential of the seeds of abundant life that are within your heart. The future is waiting for you!

The world may challenge me, but God is for me.

See yourself as God sees you, as vital to His purpose to bless all the families of the earth! Decide to be a positive part of the future. Believe that God is for you, and through you He can shape the futures of others. Will you cooperate?

Surely blessing I will bless you, and multiplying I will multiply you (Hebrews 6:14).

That is your future if you will believe it.

ABOUT BARRY BENNETT

A graduate of Christ for the Nations Institute in Dallas, Texas, Barry has served the Lord since 1972. He and his wife, Betty Kay, ministered to Cambodian refugees in Dallas for nearly three years and served as missionaries in Mexico, Guatemala, and Chile for over 12 years. In 2001, they returned to Texas, where Barry served as director and teacher at a Spanish language Bible institute. In 2007, Barry joined Andrew Wommack Ministries.

Visit Barry at
www.barrybennett.org

and on Facebook at
www.facebook.com/officialbarrybennett/

Fast. Easy. Convenient.

For the latest Harrison House product information and author news, look no further than your computer. All the details on our powerful, life-changing products are just a click away. New releases, email subscriptions, testimonies, monthly specials—find them all in one place. Visit harrisonhouse.com today!

harrisonhouse.com

The Harrison House Vision

Proclaiming the truth and the power
of the Gospel of Jesus Christ with excellence.
Challenging Christians
to live victoriously,
grow spiritually,
know God intimately.

Connect with us on
f Facebook @ HarrisonHousePublishers
and **⊙** Instagram @ HarrisonHousePublishing
so you can stay up to date with news
about our books and our authors.

Visit us at **www.harrisonhouse.com**
for a complete product listing as well as
monthly specials for wholesale distribution.